Dear Teacher

William H. Peltz

Dear Teacher

Expert Advice for Effective Study Skills

CORWIN PRESS
A SAGE Publications Company
Thousand Oaks, CA 91320

For information:

Corwin Press
A Sage Publications Company
2455 Teller Road
Thousand Oaks, California 91320
www.corwinpress.com

Sage Publications India Pvt Ltd
B 1/I 1 Mohan Cooperative
Industrial Area
Mathura Road, New Delhi 110 044
India

Sage Publications Ltd.
1 Oliver's Yard
55 City Road
London EC1Y 1SP
United Kingdom

Sage Publications Asia-Pacific Pte Ltd
33 Pekin Street #02-01
Far East Square
Singapore 048763

Printed in the United States of America

Library of Congress Cataloging-in-Publication Data

Peltz, William H.

Dear teacher: Expert advice for effective study skills/William H. Peltz.
    p. cm.
Includes bibliographical references and index.
ISBN 978-1-4129-3882-2 (cloth)
ISBN 978-1-4129-3883-9 (pbk.)
    1. Study skills. 2. Homework. 3. Test-taking skills. I. Title.

LB1049.P417 2007
373.13'0281—dc

222006101264

This book is printed on acid-free paper.

07   08   09   10   11   10   9   8   7   6   5   4   3   2   1

Acquisitions Editor:	Allyson P. Sharp
Editorial Assistant:	Nadia Kashper
Production Editor:	Libby Larson
Copy Editor:	Teresa Herlinger
Typesetter:	C&M Digitals (P) Ltd.
Proofreader:	Dorothy Hoffman
Cover Designer:	Rose Storey
Graphic Designer:	Lisa Miller

Contents

Preface

Studying is what we do in order to learn about subjects, regardless of whether they are those that are taught in school or that we learn on our own. Study skills have to do with the *way* we study. For the most part, students learn many of their study skills through a process of trial and error, rather than in any formal, structured way. These skills may have met most of the academic demands in grade school, but starting around the seventh grade, things change. Courses become more abstract, begin to move at a faster pace, and cover more material. Increasingly, students find they are expected to be independent, self-sufficient learners.

Some students enter school thinking they know how to study. They are bright, they have been academically successful, and they earned pretty good marks in earlier grades. Then they take their first test, and they do not earn the grade to which they had become accustomed. Those old study techniques no longer work quite so well. Suddenly, some of them even seem to be inefficient or inadequate; they just cannot keep up with the new, higher academic demands. Still other skills that are now needed were never learned. Some students will successfully adapt, but many—probably most—will need varying amounts of help. They need to be shown new, more effective ways to study.

Because you are reading this book, it is safe to assume that you are not happy with the way your students are studying and that you want to help them. Perhaps you sense something is not working for a specific student but cannot quite identify the problem because you have never considered all of the individual, yet intermeshed, strategies that fall under the banner of "study skills." Maybe you realize that learning study skills by trial and error just does not work in today's fast-paced world. You want to demonstrate some skills to your class, but you only know a few. This book is designed to help you realign your students' existing study skills and to introduce others. My intent is to give you strategies that will help the learner to cope successfully with those newer, more difficult courses. I will introduce you to some very powerful study skills that can be used in every discipline and throughout life, as students become lifelong learners. First and foremost, I, like you, am a classroom teacher. I am not about to give you skills that exist in some abstract realm that is unconnected to what you and I experience in our classrooms; I use all of these skills with my students, and they work.

I had middle school teachers in mind as a primary audience as I wrote this book. It is in those grades that students learn so many fundamental skills, whether they are physical (how to play a sport and work as a member of a team) or behavioral (how to treat others and themselves). While middle school children learn many academic skills (how to perform various math functions; write a well designed, cogent paragraph; think like a historian; or speak another language), they are rarely taught the skills of studying. Students are left to discover them on their own. That is unfortunate because time is just too short and today's academic demands have become too great. Students often do not find the requisite skills without help; this book is designed to enable you to give that help.

Teachers who work beyond the middle school grades will also benefit from learning the lessons I offer. I taught high school biology for the first 15 years of my career, and as I taught that subject, I would also help students improve their note-taking or test-preparation skills. I watched as they gained confidence and became more proficient scholars. I truly realized I was on the right track when one girl dramatically raised her test scores by more than 30 points! Through experiences such as these, I began to sense that my real job was to teach more than just subject matter.

These strategies can be taught in a number of venues. I weave study skills into my science classes throughout the year. For example, I might demonstrate how to annotate a text when I give out the first assignment of the year. The history teacher can advise students about how best to prepare for essay questions when the class is reviewing for an upcoming test. Appropriate note-taking skills can be explored by the English teacher when the class discusses the symbolism in a novel. Teaching study skills in context is natural, and the students will be much more receptive and amenable to learning them when they are introduced this way.

Small, extra-help groups or tutorial sessions are also ideal environments for imparting study skills. I even teach study skills when I hold parent conferences. I often ask the student to be present with the parents. I probe into how the student studies, explore how the parents are involved in the process, and then offer suggestions. In each case, whether I am instructing a class, working with an individual, or helping a family, I teach the technique and explain why it works. I start by summarizing what the student is doing. For example, in a parent conference, I might say to the student, "Let me see if I have this right. You study for your test the night before, after you have done your other homework. You read over your notes until you feel you know them. You then have your mother or father quiz you, and you seem to know the material. But when you take the test, you do poorly. You no longer seem to know anything, and now you are really frustrated." I want to verify that I understand the problem, and I also want to convey the message that I empathize with the student and really want to help. Then I offer a "diagnosis." In this case, I would say, "There are several things that we will work on that will help you, but what stands out is that you are not giving yourself a chance to memorize, to internalize the material. You are only becoming *familiar* with it." I want to establish that I recognize the problem, that I know how to solve it, and that I have become a partner with the student. I would then explain how we think information becomes stored in long-term memory and why it is so easily forgotten if it is not properly consolidated. My intent is to give the student and parents enough information so that studying is no longer a mystery and to suggest that doing well on tests is not just a matter of chance. I want them to be able to understand why the techniques I am about to recommend really do work. I want to empower them, and I want to increase the likelihood that the student will be able to grow.

Some students need a few simple tune-ups while others need more in the way of major overhauls. Over the many years I have worked in classrooms, I have encountered very few students who did not want to succeed; they just did not know what to do. Oh, they knew the right phrases—"I just need to take good notes," "I should listen more carefully," or "I should start using study cards"—but they rarely knew how to translate those catchwords into practice. At best, they were studying inefficiently; at worst, they had serious gaps in their study skills. They were left to their own devices . . . and they were floundering. Sadly, they were not earning the grades that were commensurate with their abilities, and they were becoming discouraged.

Middle school is the perfect time to begin to learn better study strategies. The brains of most elementary school children are not developed well enough to handle much more than the most basic skills, but by middle school, those brains are far enough along in the maturation process and are ready to learn these more sophisticated techniques (Carraway, 2003).

Incorporating new study strategies into an existing behavioral framework is not easy. A few students might try one or two skills for a while, but in all probability, they will revert to their old, ineffective ways after the novelty wears off. Changing behaviors is hard to do. Although we can, and should, teach study techniques to large groups, the lessons are more likely to be internalized when we work one-on-one with a student, providing ongoing support. But I am a full-time teacher and cannot give lengthy, individual attention to every student every day (although I will make sure a student who has trouble remembering to turn in homework has done so and give praise as it is submitted, or walk by another student and ask how the study schedule is coming along. These brief, focused connections provide powerful reinforcement). For that reason, I strongly believe in collaborating with a coach: usually a parent or guardian who understands the skill and to whom the student must report on a regular basis. This person needs to provide positive reinforcement and encouragement during those fragile, early days when the new skill feels awkward and is most likely to be abandoned. It is easier to keep repeating a skill until it has been internalized if the student works in partnership with an adult.

Just as we are awkward at first when we learn a new skill on the playing field, we stumble and make mistakes when we learn a new study skill. The coach's role is to help the student move through this beginning stage and to give support so the student will not feel he or she is a failure. The coach becomes the student's temporary source of self-discipline during this learning period. Through conversation, the coach provides positive, constructive feedback so the student can see more clearly how the new study skills help. The coach stays with the student until the new skill becomes an internalized behavior, a habit. I frequently talk with the student, and I stay in constant contact with the coach, too. I ask the parent-coach to check in with me every few weeks, and I notify the coach of changes I observe in class. Learning new skills involves a true partnership.

My second audience consists of those people who will act as coaches. I hope parents who want to help their children will read this book, especially if they are going to take on the role of the coach. Parents and study skill coaches need to understand each skill and understand how the strategies I discuss complement each other.

I like the way students talk about studying. They are delightfully honest about their feelings, so I used their own words to introduce each topic, writing as if a student had sent a letter to an advice column. For the most part, I answered the letters the way I talk to students in order to model what I say when I talk about study skills. I well remember when I was asked questions like those in this book in my first few years of teaching. I frequently fumbled for an appropriate response. I hope some of these questions sound familiar and that my responses help you add to your own repertoire of teaching strategies. I also hope this approach makes this book more interesting for you because, let's face it, studying is not the most riveting subject.

The letters are grouped in sections, starting with an introductory, general section. It is really foundational and sets the stage for the other sections. In it, I explore the barriers that block growth. Even though deep inside, children may want to change, they sometimes find it hard to take that frightening first step. After confronting those obstacles, I explain why we need a coach. In the second section, I look at those skills and strategies associated with organizing notebooks and taking notes. Too often, we teachers are unaware just how difficult it is to take notes, and I offer several suggestions that will help students in this task. The next section is devoted to an examination of homework. I give tips on how to keep track of assignments, suggest where homework should be done, and give advice about the construction of a study schedule. In addition, I explore ways in which to read informational textbooks. Test preparation and test-taking strategies are examined in the fourth section. I devote the last section to exams because they are unique, as tests go, and they need to be approached a bit differently.

I know some skills could have been placed in more than one section, and that is one reason why you should read all of the letters. While I recommend that you read these letters in order, you can also pick and choose, jumping around to find those skills that you need to learn first. But you will find that each skill is connected to other skills. They complement and reinforce each other, working together to maximize the efficiency and effectiveness with which a student learns. For that reason, you might just want to begin at the beginning.

While some of the strategies I mention have been around for decades, others are new. Our understanding of how the brain functions and how we learn is changing at an incredible rate. Research has explained why some of those old strategies work so well and has also revealed entirely new ways to study. At times I refer to how the brain works because the more students understand how they learn and why a specific study skill works, the more likely they will be willing to try out and practice that strategy.

Do these techniques work? Will the results be worth the effort? The answer is yes, to both questions. Some strategies are fairly easy to learn, while others will be harder. Some techniques will result in immediate (or almost immediate) improvement, while others will take longer before they begin to work. But effective study strategies do work. How much improvement you will see depends on many factors: how well the students like the subject (it is much harder to learn a subject we do not particularly enjoy), their state of mental and physical well-being (it is harder to study when we do not feel well or when we are tired), and how easily they learn. Some students can memorize relatively quickly, while others need much more time to get the same material locked into their brains. In other words, not everyone who employs these study strategies eventually gets an A+ average, so I won't hold out any false expectations. Nevertheless, there will be improvement, and that should be the goal we set for our students.

That said, improved grades should not be our only goal. Study skills teach organization, which gives us greater control over our lives. Giving students this kind of power should also be a noteworthy reason to teach study skills. The organizational skills that they learn now will help them throughout their lives.

Teaching study skills is hard work; it requires tremendous patience, tenacity, and sensitivity. We need to realize how hard it is to change a behavior. What does it take to change study strategies? The answer is a very strong desire and some real effort. Very few changes involve a quick fix. There is no silver bullet; changing study habits requires hard work on the part of students. The student has to *want* to change, and be willing to stick with it; he or she even has to be willing to give up some freedoms. Most students had more freedom when they did not study effectively. They just glossed over their work, so they had more time to play. Some barely went through the motions when they did an assignment, so they didn't tax their brains too much. Now they are going to have to sweat a little and spend more time at their studies. The question is, are they willing to make the kind of effort required to learn more effective study strategies? Will they persevere, even if the new techniques feel a bit awkward at first and do not produce immediate improvement? Will they keep trying a new strategy, even if it takes them a bit longer to do their work for the first few weeks? Do they have the courage to try new things?

There used to be a saying in the garment district in New York City: "Ya don't get nuttin' fer nuttin'." Students will not develop more effective study strategies unless they make a real and sustained effort. Most students cannot do this alone; they will need someone who becomes a partner in the process. In addition to teaching the study skill, you have to become that partner, supporting and inspiring the student. If you are willing to give this a try, read on. I think you will be thrilled by what you learn and by the gifts that you will be able to give your students, and I am honored to be part of the journey you are about to undertake.

ACKNOWLEDGMENTS

Have you ever seen a flock of Canada geese flying overhead? One goose always flies in the lead position at the center of the V-formation. The other geese spread out behind, each honking its support for the leader, ready to help if needed. The lead goose must feel that sense of partnership, and I suspect it flies all the better for it. Being the lead goose is not unlike writing a book. Authors do not write alone; many people become involved in it, lending their encouragement, support, and expertise, and helping the author to succeed. Among the many people who have helped me are those in the school where I work. In that incredible place, I developed my craft and finally discovered the more spiritual nature of teaching. If we strip away all of its distractions, we find that, at its core, teaching is an act of love. I thank the thousands of students with whom I have worked and from whom I have learned, and I am grateful to the many teachers from around the world who openly and willingly shared their experiences and strategies.

I very much appreciate the kind words of David Griswold, K. Michael Hibbard, and Lucy Martin, who willingly and graciously read an early draft of this book, and I value the conversations we had along the way. I am grateful to Dr. David Mullins, who kindly provided the MRIs and was so supportive. The following reviewers gave many insightful, helpful, and much-appreciated suggestions for the improvement of my manuscript; their comments revealed them as master teachers:

Lisa Gaines
Teacher, English/Language Arts
Homewood City Schools
Homewood, AL

Toni Ramey
Secondary Science Teacher
Mobile County Public School System
Mobile, AL

Harriett J. Tillett
Assistant Principal for Curriculum and Instruction
Person High School
Roxboro, NC

Nadia Kashper, my editorial assistant at Corwin Press, has been a true ally. She renewed my energy each time she e-mailed to ask how things were coming along, and her orchestration of all the elements that have gone into making this book has been masterful. Allyson Sharp became my editor just before I submitted the final manuscript, and her warmth instantly made me feel very much a part of the Corwin family.

A copy editor is a very special person. Not only does she have to catch any errors that appear in a manuscript, but she has to develop an acute empathy for the style and personality of the author as she makes suggestions for improvement. Teresa Herlinger has done this magnificently.

Every day while working on this project, I mentally thanked my wife, Neville, for her suggestions and patience, as well as for creating an environment at home that allowed me to immerse myself in this book. If I failed to express my gratitude enough times directly to her, I do so now in this more public forum.

About the Author

 **William H. Peltz** started his teaching career at the Greenwich Academy in Connecticut in 1971, where he weaved his knowledge of study skills into his high school general science, biology, and advanced placement biology courses. He was a consultant to that school's ninth-grade study skills program and was the chairman of the science department before moving to its middle school, where he taught sixth- and seventh-grade science and, for a while, was that division's assistant head. He currently teaches seventh-grade science and is an advisor. In addition to writing for science teachers, he gives workshops about science teaching techniques and lectures about the application of brain research to the classroom.

PART I

Overcoming Obstacles and Negative Attitudes

Our goal should be to help our students grow up and accept responsibility for their own actions, but that is not easy for everyone. Sometimes, we have to set the stage before we actually begin to teach study skills. In this section, therefore, I confront those negative attitudes that block the student from taking that first, sometimes scary leap. I explain why homework and studying is important, and I recommend that the student work closely with an adult, a coach. Effective study coaches give encouragement and nurture students through this process of growth, reducing their sense of risk and increasing the likelihood that they will experience positive behavioral change.

I feel compelled to give a word of caution. Practicing sound study strategies and developing a positive, I'm-in-charge-of-my-life attitude does not guarantee that a student will receive an A+. Nevertheless, these strategies really do help. Students will experience improved organizational skills, increased comprehension while reading a text, and a more powerful ability to remember. I've seen many students who, over the course of time, learned how to become more effective learners. Your students may not earn the highest grades, but they will see improvement.

1

Stinkin' Thinkin' and Other Roadblocks

Dear Teacher,

I've been told I engage in "Stinkin' Thinkin'." It doesn't sound good. What does it mean?

Sincerely,

PU

Dear PU,

Have your ever heard a classmate say, "It was the teacher's fault I blew that test. He asked the wrong questions"? This is what is known as *stinkin' thinkin'*. It results in *toxic behavior,* causing us to behave in ways that undermine us and make matters worse. Stinkin' thinkin' is a way of thinking that makes no sense; after all, other students earned good scores on that test, so the questions weren't "wrong" for them. Stinkin' thinkin' and toxic behavior block growth. If you engage in them, you are not accepting responsibility for your own behavior.

If you use stinkin' thinkin', you are playing the blame game. It is a behavioral defense mechanism called projection (see Figure 1.1). You might have done poorly on the test, but it is easier not to accept responsibility and to blame someone or something else ("It was the teacher's fault. The questions weren't on the review sheet."). When you project, you put the responsibility for your behavior onto others to protect your self-image. You are really saying it is psychologically easier for you to blame others than to admit that you have weaknesses and faults.

Perhaps I can make my point clear by referencing a letter another student wrote. In it, she claimed her teacher was boring. This is my response:

> Lack of interest makes success in school so much more difficult. But the fact is, you do not get points back on low grades just because you find the teacher to be less than stimulating. You might get a little bit of sympathy from one or two people, but not much, and the chances are they are just being polite.
>
> What you are doing is called projection. You are saying it was somebody else's fault—the boring teacher, the boring class, the boring textbook. You are projecting the problem onto others. I am not denying you find your class to be boring (and maybe I would even agree with you!), but let me share an important lesson about life. You cannot change others—in this case, your teacher. You cannot change the class or the textbook or the subject or the way the test was

written. You can, however, change yourself. You have to learn how to succeed despite your feelings. Face the problem and find ways to overcome it; do not run away from it.

Figure 1.1   Three of the most common study skill–related defense mechanisms a student might use. By asking questions ("How did everyone else do on the test?" or "Whose responsibility is it to catch up after an absence?"), the teacher begins to weaken the defense mechanism, which gives the teacher an opportunity to intervene and to begin the process of change.

COMMON STUDENT DEFENSE MECHANISMS		
DEFENSE MECHANISM	**DEFINITION**	**EXAMPLE**
Avoidance	Works around having to face a situation that is painful	The student is always absent on the day of the test; the student "forgets" to show up for an appointment with the teacher when the subject is the student's failing grades.
Projection	Blames the behavior on someone else, when in truth it was the student's responsibility	"The teacher just doesn't like me," or "The teacher asked the wrong questions."
Rationalization	Gives a *seemingly* logical explanation for a behavior as opposed to the *real* reason	"I was absent when that topic was taught," which fails to acknowledge the fact that it was the student's responsibility to catch up on the work.

PU, if you are blaming your teacher because you failed, I bet, deep inside, you know who really failed the test. Now you have a conflict, and this produces guilt. The problem is that you do not know how to do better on your tests. That leads to more projection and more guilt. I bet you are even becoming discouraged and resentful.

If this description is accurate, you are in a rut. You are getting bad grades, but you do not know how to improve them.

Your self-image deteriorates, making success even more unlikely. You engage in negative behaviors—stinkin' thinkin' and toxic behavior—but do not know how to be more constructive and positive.

If you engage in stinkin' thinkin', it is time for you to accept responsibility for your own behavior. Admit that your poor test grades are no one else's fault but your own. Growing up involves learning how to accept responsibility. Having decided to do that, you should next decide that you want to learn how to improve those grades. Find a study strategy that you think will help and practice it. Then add another strategy to your repertoire. Keep building your skills and soon you will be on your way to better study habits and higher test grades.

That you wrote this letter and are reaching for the answer tells me you are ready to change. A positive attitude is so very important. It motivates you to find new ways to study, and it also makes other people want to help you. You will find that each time you practice and internalize a new skill, learning the next new skill becomes easier. As you begin to see results from your effort, your positivism and self-confidence will strengthen. Growing up is a journey, and you have decided to gain some understanding and to assume control of a part of it. Have a great trip!

2

My Homework
Is Boring

Dear Teacher,

Homework is boring! How can I make it more interesting?

Sincerely,

Bored Stiff

Dear Bored,

I like your attitude. You want to overcome a problem that you are facing. Yes, sometimes homework *is* boring, and for any number of reasons. It is at times like this that we have to force ourselves to sit down and get on with it. Your question actually gives you the answer—it is really all about making your work more interesting.

There are a few strategies that you can utilize to increase your interest in your homework. You need to know that researchers are beginning to think that the brains of today's students are wired differently from the brains of people who were in school 40 years ago. The reason has to do with technology (Healey, 1990). Today, television shows and movies have a much faster pace. Computers provide almost instantaneous feedback. Children play an enormous number of video games in which scenes change constantly and rapidly. None of this was happening several decades ago. We know that our brain cells connect with each other in response to our experiences. If we play the violin, for example, the brain cells associated with the thumb and pinky finger of our left hand, the fingering digits, have many more connections than we would see in the brain of a person who is not a musician (Ratey, 2000; Schlaug, Jancke, & Pratt, 1995). Our experiences determine how our brain cells connect with each other. Because students have watched a lot of television and played many computer video games, their brains are wired for fast-paced activities. What you need to do is change your approach to learning so it appeals to your contemporary brain. It should not surprise you to learn that the U.S. Army uses computer games to train its young soldiers (Lenoir & Lowood, n.d.). Some of the strategies you need to use to make homework more interesting revolve around games and pacing.

Find a way to turn your homework into a game. Pretend you are the teacher. As you do your homework, figure out how you could make it more interesting to your imaginary students. How would you explain a particular concept to them? How would you teach it to someone about two years younger than yourself? To do this successfully, you not only have to understand the concept, but you also need to explain it in simpler terms (that is always a good test to see if you understand it). Find an example of the concept you are studying that would appeal to your friends. Pretend you are some other student. How would that person do the homework? Pretend you are peer tutoring a friend. How would you explain the homework in an interesting and meaningful way?

You cannot change the speed at which you learn, but you can use movement to create a rhythm while you recite what you have learned. Many students sit at their desk while they prepare their study cards. When they are ready to memorize and test themselves, they stand up and walk back and forth, pacing as they recite what they have learned. Their movement sets the tempo, or pace, which helps their brains concentrate on what they have learned. In addition, they are activating a part of the brain called the cerebellum.

Figure 2.1   The prefrontal cortex of the frontal lobe, the amygdala, and the cerebellum in the right hemisphere of the brain.

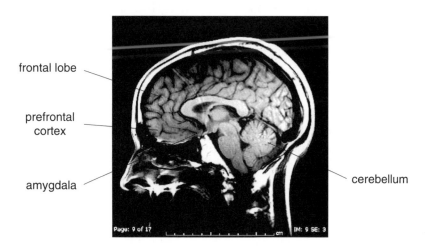

SOURCE: MRI Courtesy of Greenwich Hospital.

Scientists used to think the cerebellum was involved only in balance and movement. Recently, however, they learned it has many connections with those parts of the brain in which we store the material we are memorizing (Wolfe, 2001b). It also has many connections with the front of the brain, an area that is responsible for controlling the memory and recall processes. Brain scientists are beginning to think there are profound links between movement and learning (Bower & Parsons, 2003). Try standing up and moving when you memorize. It works!

Studying for classes we like is easier. The reason has to do with a part of your brain called the amygdala. It responds to emotion (Cahill & McGaugh, 1995; Cahill, Prins, Weber, & McGaugh, 1994; Greenleaf & Levine, 2001; LeDoux, 1996). It will zero in on anything that interests you, on something that is fun or humorous. The amygdala primes the learning process and makes memorizing easier. Find ways to make your homework a bit more fun. The amygdala also likes novelty—something new. So try out a few new study skills. Change the way you study. You need to create ways of learning that appeal to your amygdala.

Having said this, there are times when even the most exciting subject can become difficult to learn. Effective study strategies give us a sense of self-discipline and organization that help us through these times. This book will help you to learn those techniques.

3

Who Has Time for Homework?

Dear Teacher,

I don't have time to do my homework. I play on the school squash team, practice my violin, take acting lessons, and play on the town hockey team. I get home late. I have chores to do at home, I eat dinner with my family, and I need to talk with my friends so I don't lose them. I don't seem to have any free time anymore. What am I supposed to do?

Sincerely,

Overloaded

Dear Overloaded,

As you rise in grade levels, it is true that the amount of homework you are expected to do each night increases. As a result, you have less time to play. Although play is important, the opportunity to engage in it does not come as often as the child in all of us would like. Learning to accept this is part of growing up. I think, however, you will discover you can find the time to complete your homework and still do other things that give you pleasure.

Having said that, I have to wonder how effectively you are using your time when you study. You should examine your study strategies. Ask yourself how effectively you are using your time. Read some of the strategies I write about in other letters, especially those about schedules. Try them out. I think you will find you will still have time left to play.

There is another element that you and I need to explore. Some students do too much. They are over-scheduled. Perhaps they do this to be more attractive to admissions committees at colleges or other schools. Perhaps they really just enjoy these activities. In any event, they lose sight of the burden that can be created when too many activities are added to the schedule. Some students can handle more activities than others; we are not created equal. Having many commitments is fine, as long as the student can also do well in school. Keep in mind that if your school record is weak, few people will care that you were on the ice hockey rink every morning at 5:00 or that you attended ballet class until 7:00 four nights a week.

I am as much, if not more concerned about the skills you may not be learning. You can probably learn the facts that you have been missing in future courses, but if you do not learn those skills now, you will find opportunities will be closed to you. If you do not learn all of the math skills that are being introduced now, for example, you might be barred from enrolling in advanced mathematics classes in the years to come. Are all of your out-of-school activities worth closing those doors?

You were not forced to do all of these things. So I have to ask: does the word *priorities* mean anything to you? You are doing too many things. One of the painful lessons some of us need to learn is that we cannot do everything, at least not right away or all at once. Perhaps you can postpone some activities. Do you take acting in school? If so, you could put off taking those acting lessons until the school holidays. Maybe you will have to drop an activity. It might be something you enjoy, but you need to keep in mind that doing your homework to the best of your ability should be one of your highest priorities.

Through the sixth grade, you were probably able to do all of your schoolwork and have fun doing a number of out-of-school activities. But starting in the seventh grade, school work changed. More work was given to you and more was expected of you. You no longer had the time to do all the things you used to do. Your life has become more complicated, and you will have to adjust. If you don't, your school work could suffer.

Talk with your parents about your schedule and its impact upon your work at school. They can help you plan your time so you can do your homework and still manage to do most of those other activities. For example, they might suggest that you practice your violin at the end of the evening for a set length of time, after you have completed your homework, instead of as soon as you come home, when the tendency might be to give yourself a bit more time on the instrument. Write out a schedule (see my letter to Hoping for Ideas about homework schedules in Chapter 20). Map out the time you will need to do all of your homework. Then add those other activities around that schedule. Talk with your parents periodically so all of you can assess how well the schedule is working. You will have to refine it as you go along, and both you and your parents need to be partners in the process.

4

Just Add Water—Skill Development Takes Time

Dear Teacher,

How long will it take me to learn these effective study strategies? I want instant results.

Sincerely,

Impatient

Dear Impatient,

I would be lying if I said study strategies don't take more time, especially at first, while you are trying to get used to them and are probably performing them a bit awkwardly. But they don't take that much more time. And the point is, as these effective study strategies are performed more efficiently, you will be learning more efficiently. Many students discover that, because they have been learning more efficiently every day and know how to memorize, their grades improve. They think more time spent studying is worth the effort when they see significant improvements in their test scores.

You can learn some strategies very quickly. Others take longer. And some take a lot longer, years in fact. But that is because it takes years to grow up. The front part of your brain, the part behind your forehead called the prefrontal cortex, is responsible for organizing information (Goldberg, 2003; Wolfe, 2003; Yurgelun-Todd, 1999). It allows you to put ideas in sequential order, it is involved in sustaining attention and focusing on a task, and it plays a role in moving information into long-term memory. Your teachers call these jobs *executive functions*. The prefrontal cortex is also the part of the brain that is involved with these sophisticated study skills that I want to share with you. It begins to come online, working in an adult way, starting around the age of 9 or 10, but it is not fully functional until age 22 in females and 25 in males (Goldberg, 2003). This means that you can begin to learn these skills immediately. Just as you can learn how to play a sport now, but won't be fully coordinated for a few more years, you can learn a study skill now, but it may take several years for that skill to mature. Just as you will be a better player on a team if you start to learn the skills of the sport now, you will be a better student if you start learning study skills right away.

So pick one or two strategies to start with, perhaps those that are most important or most desperately needed. Practice them for a couple of weeks, and then add another strategy. Practice it and then choose another. Use the KISS approach (Keep It Short and Simple). If you take on too many strategies

Figure 4.1   Executive functions of the prefrontal cortex (Barkley, 2000; Zelago, 2005)

Ability to consider consequences
Attentiveness and focusing on task
Motivation
Organizational skills
    Breaking tasks into manageable units
    Ordering tasks
Self-monitoring
Sequencing
Time management
    Planning ahead
    Time perception
Working memory
Transfer from working to long-term memory

at once, or if you do not give yourself time to practice the new skills and develop new study habits, you will be overwhelmed and will not have as much success.

I recommend you practice a strategy for at least two weeks. You need to pass beyond the stage in which it feels uncomfortable and different. Just like practicing a new skill in sports, you need to keep at it until you find you are no longer consciously practicing the skill; you need to arrive at the point at which it has been incorporated into your behavior and feels almost as natural as the way you hold your pencil.

Be patient. Learning new behaviors takes time.

5

I'm Too Tired to Study

Dear Teacher,

I feel tired much of the time. My mother yells at me because I can't wake up and get out of bed. In class, I yawn a lot and there are times when I realize I haven't been paying attention. And then I seem to find my energy at night. I wasn't like this when I was younger. What's going on?

Sincerely,

Sleepy

Dear Sleepy,

Welcome to adolescence! Teens naturally fall asleep later and wake up later because their biological clocks have changed. Furthermore, they need more sleep than they did as children. The amount of sleep that people need varies (Hobson, 2003; Wolfe, 2001a, 2003). Thomas Edison, for example, needed only four hours of sleep each night. Some adults need nine hours. Typically, teens need 9 to 11 hours of sleep a night and, when tired, can easily sleep 14 hours. Sleep researchers think this has to do with the slight increase in the release of the hormone melatonin that happens during this stage of our lives.

Teens would like to sleep until 8:00 or 9:00 every morning, if not later. Unfortunately, life does not work that way. They have to wake up early so they can be at school on time. There are only a handful of middle and secondary-level schools in this country that have changed their schedules to accommodate the biology of the adolescent. All of the other teens are stuck in a world that responds to adult needs. Most schools open at a time when parents can drop their children off on their way to work and when the buses run. Schools have to open early enough so there will still be sunlight when the afternoon games are played. Students' sleep patterns are rarely considered when the school day is planned.

As an adolescent, you can live with this society-created schedule for a while, but you pay a price. You do not get a full night of complete, restful sleep. Eventually, you become tired. People who are sleep deprived undergo change. They tune out more easily and find paying attention to be difficult. This is not a desirable state to be in during school, is it? As people lose even more sleep, their bodies' thermostats are affected and can no longer maintain a stable body temperature. They find they are chilly in a room in which others are comfortable. They do not metabolize food efficiently, so they may eat a lot, but much less of the food's energy goes into their bodies. If sleep deprivation continues, their ability to protect themselves from colds becomes affected. I am sure you are not this deprived of sleep, but the point is that loss of sleep is a real problem and can be serious.

Our brains are wonderfully active when we sleep, but in ways that are different from when we are awake. The brain does not turn off when we sleep (Society for Neuroscience, 2003). When we sleep, our ability to make decisions, think rationally, pay attention, and smell and hear is depressed, but other areas of the brain are surprisingly busy. The brain processes old information and reviews strong emotions (which explains why so many of our dreams involve powerful emotions). We still have much to learn about sleep, but we do know it is a surprisingly busy and crucial part of our day.

Another significant consequence of the adolescent shift in sleep patterns is the possibility that these students tend to remain sleepy during the day and then become active in the evening. As a result, they miss much of the school day experience. If you are one of these students, try several strategies to keep you more alert. Sit near the front of the class. Periodically, stretch and change your body position. That helps increase your circulation and brings more oxygen to your brain. Avoid lunches that are heavy in carbohydrates, which tend to relax you and make you less alert (read my letter about food for the brain that I wrote to Upscale in Chapter 39). But most important, try to get more sleep. I have talked with many teenagers who say they stay up late. They have finished their homework, but they don't feel ready to fall asleep. So they turn on the computer and chat online, often until 11:00 at night, or even later. Unfortunately, this just deprives them of more sleep.

I advise these students to develop a routine in which they stop studying each night at an appropriate hour. Drinking a glass of milk when they finish their homework causes the brain to release serotonin, a chemical that helps bring on sleep (Berkhoff, 2005). They should get into bed and read a book for pleasure for about 15 to 20 minutes in order to unwind. I do not recommend watching television or listening to the radio; it is not relaxing. Our bodies need about two weeks to adapt to a new biological rhythm, so this routine should be practiced for at least that long before you can expect to feel any change. This can then become a permanent routine. Teens should also try to regain some of their sleep on weekends. This is not a perfect solution, but it will help.

A parent coach will be useful. That person can assist you in establishing a structured environment that will help you get through this stage in your life (read my next letter, in Chapter 6). You can pick up a few more hours of sleep on the weekends and return to sleeping according to your biological clock on long holidays.

6

Get a Coach—
Your Very Own
Personal Trainer
for Studying

Dear Teacher,

I want to improve my study habits, but I can't seem to stick with it. I try a new technique and it works for a few days. But then I begin to slide back into my old habits. What can I do?

Sincerely,

Getting Frustrated

Dear Getting,

Of course you are getting frustrated. You want to change, but you do not seem to be able to. In addition to feeling annoyed with yourself, you must be feeling a little bit guilty, too.

Our brains are very interested in change, in things that are novel. Something different gets our attention. An unexpected flicker of motion seen out of the corner of our eye makes us look over in that direction. The first days of school are always more interesting than classes held a few weeks later, after everything has become routine. Electronic games are interesting, in part, because they are fast-paced and keep changing.

When you try a new study strategy, your brain is interested. But after a short time, it realizes you are asking it to work. You are telling it to stop behaving the old way, which it is used to, and to learn new behaviors. That takes effort, and your brain would prefer to go back to the old study behaviors, even though they are less effective. Learning new behaviors can take weeks, and your brain just does not want to do that.

So you have to find a way to force your brain to keep at it. One way is to find a coach. Your teachers can show you some very powerful study techniques, but you will probably need someone who can work with you every day. Most teachers have too many students and are too busy to give daily help. Your coach should be a person who wants to see you succeed, who can give you the reinforcement you need, who is knowledgeable about study skills, and who is readily available to you. A coach provides motivation, pushing you when you need it. This person needs to understand what you are trying to learn and how you are doing it so that he or she can be supportive and encouraging. A coach models the correct study behavior and then encourages you to try it. You will need to have an open and honest dialogue with your coach, sharing your strengths as well as your weaknesses, your successes and your failures. A coach also needs to ask questions so you have a chance to think about what you are doing: Are you finding it easy to change? Have you seen any benefits yet? Is this skill taking the same amount of time as it did when you first tried to practice it, i.e., are you becoming more proficient in the skill? The coach provides positive feedback and reinforcement and, when appropriate, identifies and criticizes inappropriate behavior in a nonevaluative manner. This means that the coach might point out when you slip, but should not punish you. Ideally, the coach communicates periodically with the teacher. I like to enlist the help of parents; I think they make the best coaches.

Ask one of your parents to be your coach. I suggest that you and that parent meet with your teacher in order to set up guidelines and realistic expectations. You want to become allies and work together. Tell your parent/coach what you are trying to achieve and how you plan to do it. You might consider writing a contract that specifies what you want to accomplish, what actions you will take, and what your coach will do.

Figure 6.1   An example of a contract between a student and coach. The teacher usually has to facilitate the completion of a contract and may need to be included in the contract.

Student/Coach Contract

Student's name: _____

I have a problem with:

I plan to change by:

Coach's name: _____

My coach will:

I certify that my coach and I have read, discussed, and agreed upon the information and plan contained in this contract. I agree to work cooperatively with my coach in order to improve my academic success from _____ (today's date) until _____ (end date), after which this contract can be extended or terminated, if agreed upon by both student and coach.

Student's signature: _____

Coach's signature: _____

The best learning contracts focus on one skill at a time. As you record what you plan to do, make sure you and your coach know how to measure that you are learning the skill. For example, if you have a problem remembering to bring home the correct notebook, you might agree to terminate the contract if you bring the right notebook for three consecutive weeks.

Figure 6.2   A conversation between a coach and a student who has had a problem remembering to record every assignment and where homework papers were placed after they were completed the night before.

Typical Conversation Between a Student and Coach

Coach (C):   You've finished your homework. How did it go, tonight?

Student (S):   Okay, but I had trouble finding my Current Events homework.

C: Oh, what happened?

S: Well, I had copied the assignment from the board onto my assignment pad. You know, the way we discussed. I wrote it down right away. But partway through the class, the teacher decided to change the homework, and I forgot that I had written it down in my notes. He was talking so fast that I did not have time to get my assignment pad from my bookbag. [The student is being absolutely honest about the problem.] It took me a few minutes to remember it was in my notes.

C: Well, that kind of thing does happen. Was it easy to find the assignment in your notes?

S: Oh, yeah, once I remembered where I had put it. You see, I skipped a few lines in my notes and marked it with a large arrow. I don't have Current Events again for a few days, and I wasn't going to review my notes until tomorrow during study hall.

C: I think you handled that one correctly, and I like the way you used that arrow. [The coach is supportive and gives positive feedback.] Okay, now let's check to be sure all your homework papers are in the homework folder. [The coach is reinforcing a new habit the student wants to learn.]

If you need to check in with a teacher on a regular basis, perhaps to obtain a signature at the end of the week to verify that every assignment was turned in, then the teacher needs to be included in your contract.

Figure 6.3   A bar graph that shows an improving trend in a behavior that the student is trying to learn.

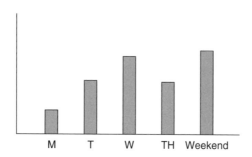

M   T   W   TH   Weekend

Agree that you have to check in with your coach regularly to report how you are coming along. You have to be honest and report your failures as well as your daily successes.

Mark your progress. You can create a bar graph that rises one square each day you stick with your new study strategy or drops a square each day you slide (see Figure 6.3). This gives you visual reinforcement.

I prefer to reward growth and positive change with praise, but you and your coach might consider creating a reward system. For each week that you successfully practice your new study skill, you could receive a small reward (maybe you could be excused from taking out the trash one night). If you slip and fail to practice your new skill, you and your coach might decide that there should be a mild punishment (perhaps you should clean out one shelf in the refrigerator during the weekend). Of course, the best rewards will be the higher grades you will start earning!

Changing old habits is not easy, and asking for help is often what it takes. So ask someone to be a coach, to share the work and to travel with you on this journey. The burden will be lighter and the chances of success far greater. Furthermore, if you stick with it, you will learn the meaning of the word perseverance and the benefits it can bring.

PART II

Notebooks and Note-Taking Skills

F or some students, the task of organizing a notebook is overwhelmingly difficult, and almost every student can improve the way in which a notebook is maintained. Note taking requires the smooth integration of numerous, complex skills. I have yet to meet the student who would not benefit from some help in these areas.

Consider the challenge young students face. The way in which they take notes differs with each subject. Science is factual, and they must record much of what the teacher says, whereas English literature involves a lot of discussion, and they need to record summaries and important ideas. Another aspect that makes note taking difficult is the students' individual learning styles. They should be properly matched to the most effective note-taking technique.

The more students practice their note-taking skills, the more adept they will become at them. They will begin to develop their own style, one that they will learn to trust.

7

Bring the Correct Notebook to Class

Dear Teacher,

I keep forgetting to bring the correct notebook to class. I'm tired of the looks I keep getting from my teachers. Do you have any easy strategies that might help me?

Sincerely,

Lookin' for Something Simple

Dear Lookin',

Luckily, there is a solution that is really quite easy: color code your classes on your schedule and use a matching color for each class notebook. Let's assume English and Math always meet back-to-back and that you keep both sets of notes in one notebook. Decide which color those courses should be. Highlight those courses on your schedule in that color and buy a notebook in the same color. Perhaps you are given so many papers in History that you need a single notebook for that course. Buy another notebook in a different color, and then use what you will come to think of as the History color to highlight that course on your schedule. Use this technique for each of your courses.

Label the outside of each binder—on the front cover *and* the spine—with the name of the course that it contains. You now have two ways of identifying your notebooks: color and course name.

Finally, put a copy of your schedule in each of your notebooks. Place another schedule inside your locker. Wherever you go, with just a quick glance, you can see what your next class is and what color notebook you need to find and bring.

Simple, isn't it? But here is the kicker: you and you alone own the responsibility to arrive at each class fully prepared with all of the appropriate materials. So get to work on it right away!

8

The How-Many-Notebooks-Do-I-Need Dilemma

Dear Teacher,

I have been told to put all my notes together in one notebook. But it seems so much easier to keep my class notes in one place, my homework papers in a folder, and notes that I take while reading my textbook and other sources in another place. Putting everything in one book seems like extra work. Why should I change?

Sincerely,

I Have 17 Notebooks!

Dear I Have,

Imagine that you have a new history textbook. You rip out all the unit and end-of-chapter questions. Then you cut out the text and put it in one notebook. You remove the pictures and diagrams and place them in a second notebook. Then you put those notations that the editors place in the margins in a third notebook, but don't even bring it to school. You keep your class notes in yet another notebook, and you keep your homework in a folder, but put the folder in a different place each day. You distribute those questions that you had ripped out in two or more notebooks, and then add the review sheet the teacher gave you for the upcoming test in any one of those notebooks. Now imagine, once you find that review sheet, you discover you have to study pages 52–78 for a test. Oh, by the way, because you had placed the folder in your math notebook, you left it at school. I know that this rather exaggerated example is absurd, but it is precisely what you are doing by maintaining several notebooks for one course. A notebook is not unlike a textbook. It should be a single, unified, well-organized study tool.

How much more efficient it would be to keep all your notes about a specific topic in a single notebook for the course. If you combine several subjects into one notebook, use divider tabs to separate the courses. You might place your class notes and handouts about the topic at the front of the notebook, followed by homework, notes from the text, and finally, any review material that pertains to that topic. Each time you begin a new topic, you begin the notes for it on a new page. In this way, your notebook will become a powerful study tool.

You won't have to go hunting for any of the material about any one topic if it has all been kept together. When students keep their papers in different notebooks or in different sections within one notebook, as you are doing, they tend to overlook one or two important papers when they study for tests, and they often fail to see how one part of the topic is connected to another. By organizing all of the parts of a topic in a single, logical, cohesive packet within one notebook, you will increase the possibility of acing your tests!

Figure 8.1   A typical organizational chart for a history class notebook.

History Notebook Organizational Chart

class notes
handouts (unless inserted in the notes)
worksheets
homework
review sheet
quiz/test

I strongly urge you to use a coach to help you organize your notebooks. Develop an organizational plan, such as the one just mentioned. Decide, for example, whether you want your homework to appear immediately after your class notes. Write out an organizational chart for your notebook.

Each time the teacher begins a new topic, you should start the first four sections of the notebook again. Tape the chart to the front inside cover so you will always remember to follow it. Then take everything out of your notebook and place each paper in its new location. If you are like some of the students I have worked with, you should also check your book bag and locker for stray papers. By the time you are done, you will have a notebook that contains everything you need.

Check in with your coach at least once a week, with your notebook in hand. Be patient; learning how to organize notebooks takes time.

"I keep my notes on my computer," I hear many students say. If you do this, make sure you *print out* your notes each day and put them in your notebook. A computer is just another notebook, and you want to combine all materials into a single notebook.

Computers offer a host of difficulties. A common problem associated with computers involves poor file management. I've lost count of the number of students who store information on their computers, only to forget where they saved it because they do not have a consistent system for saving notes. Some notes are labeled according to their subject matter while others are titled by the date on which they were taken. Your teachers will not be the least bit sympathetic if you cannot locate all of your class notes. Just because you pressed the "Save" command does not guarantee you will remember where those notes ended up if you store them in multiple places and do not know what you titled them. Get in the habit of using computer folders. You should have one folder on your computer for each course. Within one folder, keep subfolders. For example, in the English folder, you might have one subfolder for grammar exercises and another for the Shakespeare play you are reading. In the Shakespeare folder, you might keep one subfolder for notes on Act One and another for notes about Act Two. Be consistent when you name your files. If you name some of your files by the topic and others by the date you entered them, they will be harder to find. I suggest you use a combination of number and name, so your first set of notes about Act One would be titled Act One_1, the next is Act One_2, and so on.

Figure 8.2   A computer file management system in which papers are placed in subfiles, which in turn are kept within a subject file. To protect yourself in the event your computer crashes, and to optimize the effectiveness of your notebook, print out your notes every day and place them in the proper place in the notebook.

FILE	SUBFILE	CONTENTS
	Metric System	notes conversion rules homework
Science	Motion	force gravity speed acceleration velocity Newton's 1st law

Even if you do have the perfect file management system, you have one other problem: computers crash. There is always the risk that your notes will disappear. In addition to periodically saving what you are working on and backing up your files, printing out hard copies of your notes and papers and putting them in your notebook gives you an additional layer of protection. Get in the habit of printing out your notes and placing *everything* into a single notebook for each class on a daily basis. Once you get used to the system, it only takes a moment or two to maintain it each day.

This might seem like a lot of unnecessary work to you. You might earn perfectly respectable grades with your current system. But as your courses become more difficult, you run the risk of losing your notes or becoming confused because your notes do not form a cohesive whole. Consequently, you will not earn those grades that match up with your ability.

There is one more reason why it is a smart idea to put all notes in a single notebook. You might know where everything is right now, but will you be able to put your fingers on everything a few months from now, when you have to get ready for exams? The chances are, you can remember your system for the unit test, but after a while, you will begin to forget where you put some of the papers.

You might have heard the phrase, "You can lead a horse to water but you cannot make him drink." Nowhere in the world of study strategies have I found this to be more true than in the organization of a notebook. The question you must answer is this: do you want to stand there and continue to do what you have always done, or do you want to drink from the trough?

9
Note-Taking Formats

Dear Teacher,

When I take notes, I just write down everything I can. Is this a good approach?

Sincerely,

Now Write This Down

Dear Now,

Some teachers tell students to record as much as they can in class, especially in very factual classes like science. Other teachers advise students to summarize and record only the key ideas. To some extent, the way we take notes reflects the field we are studying. I think we have to learn several ways to take notes and then use the approach that is best suited for the class we are in as well as for the particular moment. Sometimes, you should use an outline format; at other times, a graphic form will work better.

There are four methods I recommend for note taking. The first is the *paragraph method*. The student records everything in a paragraph format. The paragraph may be as short as a phrase or may consist of many lines of information. Each time a new subject is introduced, a line is skipped and a new paragraph is begun.

Figure 9.1   The paragraph method for taking notes.

Inertia is the tendency of an object that is at rest to remain at rest and the tendency of an object that is moving to continue to move in the same direction. An example may be a book that is resting on the desk. It will continue to sit there. It has inertia. It does not want to "go" anywhere on its own. Another example is an ice skater who is gliding along on the ice in a straight line. She will continue to glide in the same direction.

What causes a change in the tendency of an object to continue doing what it is doing? What can overcome inertia? An opposing force such as friction. It will cause the ice skater to slow down and stop.

This technique records all of the information that will be needed, but there are two drawbacks to this note-taking method. You have to be able to write really fast so as not to miss anything, and the notes are hard to review. Nothing stands out. It is hard to see the relationship of one piece of information to another. I recommend that this method be used sparingly.

The second method, called the *mapping method,* relates one fact or concept to another; it uses a combination of brief notes and graphic connectors. It is a diagrammatic way of taking notes. Most people suggest writing the main idea in the center of the page, but I have never found that to be very practical. I am less concerned with *where* I put the main point than in *identifying* it, so I circle it. Then I place all of the information that is related to that idea in boxes. I connect those boxes to the main idea in ways that are meaningful. If I were to use the same information that I gave you for the paragraph method, but took notes using the mapping method instead, I would have circled the main idea, which is the definition of inertia. I would put each example in a separate box and draw lines to each of them from the circled definition. I would put the information about friction in another box and connect it with a line to the ice skater box. The mapping method not only gives me a record of everything that the teacher said, but it also provides a powerful way to see how everything is related.

Figure 9.2   The mapping method for taking notes.

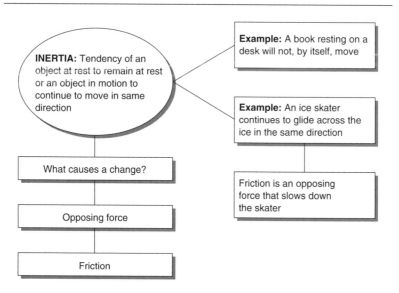

This system requires you to think constantly about the content of the lesson as it is given, recognizing how the various parts of the lecture are connected. That kind of interaction strengthens your understanding of the class. The visual component also makes reviewing your notes a much easier task. This method is harder to use when the teacher is not well organized or when you do not see where the class is headed. You may find you use this method for a portion of your notes, and then switch to another method. That is entirely appropriate.

The third method borrows from the format of an outline and is called the *outline method* (although it is not a true outline). The first sentence or two begins at the left margin and contains the main idea. Supporting facts are indented and listed under the first sentence. An example of a fact would be indented again. Because indentation is used, numbers, letters, or Roman numerals commonly used in a true outline are not needed, although they are sometimes helpful, especially when you are taking notes of lists. For example, imagine that your English teacher has been talking about amusing poetry. Your notes might look like this:

Fun and silly poems:

1. "The Purist" by Ogden Nash
2. "Tender-Heartedness" by Harry Graham
3. "The Naught Preposition" by Morris Bishop
4. "Slithergadee" by Shel Silverstein

Outlining records both content and relationships, and it produces well-organized notes. The outline method is more powerful than the paragraph method because you do not have to write as much, so you are less likely to miss parts of what the teacher said. Also, it is much easier to read than a paragraph. That is important when you have to go back to review your notes.

The fourth method is called the *Cornell method* (or the *Cornell note-taking method* or the *Cornell system*). This method provides a systematic method for condensing and summarizing notes

Figure 9.3   The outline method for taking notes.

Inertia is tendency of an object to remain at rest or
continue in motion
    If at rest, will continue at rest
        Example: book on table
    If moving, will continue to move in same direction
        at same speed forever
    Example: ice skater gliding across ice
        Stays in straight line and continues gliding
        This situation will not change until an
        opposing force acts on the skater
    Friction opposes skater, causing her to slow down

without recopying. It is a simple, efficient method that saves time. It has also been called the "Do-it-right-in-the-first-place" system (Carraway, 2003), and that tells you that this is a powerful technique.

Figure 9.4 illustrates the formatting for the Cornell system. A horizontal line should be drawn 2 inches from the bottom. This space is the Summary section. A vertical line should be drawn 2½ inches from the left margin of the paper. This is the Review column. The remaining space to the right is the Note-Taking Area.

Take notes in the Note-Taking Area. In this section, record what the teacher says. Use the paragraph method, mapping method, outline method, or any combination of these techniques. Later, after class, as you read over your notes, you will complete the other two sections on the page. In the Review column, write the key words or phrases that appear in the notes. Reduce the notes to just a word or a phrase or two. Record key questions in this section in order to clarify your thinking about difficult concepts or ideas. As you learn how to use the Review column, you will find that it gives you some good study card material. In the Summary section, write a sentence or two that captures the main idea of all the notes about a particular topic. What were they all about? In Figure 9.5, I used the Cornell method to record those science notes we have been considering.

Figure 9.4   The Cornell method for taking notes.

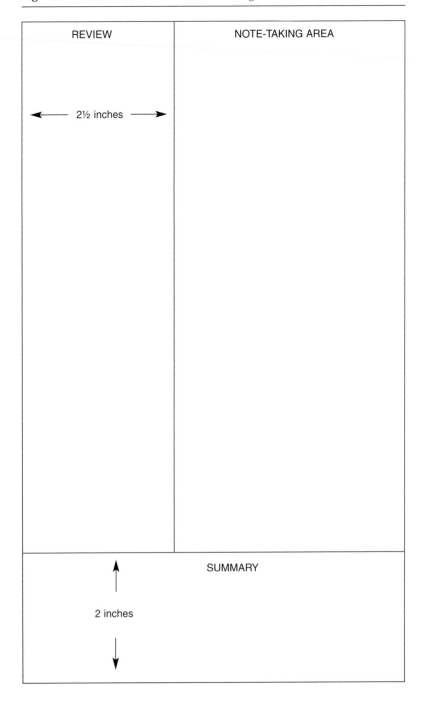

Figure 9.5   An example of how the Cornell method might be used.

Inertia	Inertia is the tendency of an object to remain at rest or to continue moving until it is acted upon by another force.
Examples	Ex: book on table stays on table until pushed Ex: skater continues gliding in same direction at same speed until friction slows her down

Introduction to Inertia/Newton's First Law

   tendency of an object to keep doing what it is doing

The Cornell system allows you to take notes using one or more of the methods I already described. It also provides you with space to record your reflections and thoughts as you review your notes at night (see my letter in Chapter 24, Brief Nightly Review of Notes).

If you review your notes each night, you will be more likely to remember what the teacher said in class. A quick, nightly review begins the process of entering the information into your long-term memory, and that makes studying for the test just a little bit easier. Keeping up with your nightly review is important. If your schedule is overly full and you cannot review your notes one night (perhaps because you need all the time you can get to study for a test), do not put off this review for more than 48 hours. Do it the very next day.

There is an additional benefit to reviewing each night. As you look over your notes, you may discover something that you really do not understand as well as you thought you did when you sat in class. You should mark this material and bring it up in class the next day. It is better to discover this now so that you can ask your teacher for help than to find out the night before the test that there is a huge gap in your knowledge, when it is too late to do anything.

I do have some strategies that apply to all styles of note taking. For example, when you take notes, first write a title or heading. Skip a line and then begin to take your notes. Knowing what the notes are about will be very helpful when you start to review. Before you write a new heading, skip a few lines. Leaving a blank line or two between sections will make your notes easier to read when you return to them. White space is very important. Notes that are crowded together are hard to read. When you begin an entirely new topic, move to a new page, write the new title or heading, and begin your next set of notes.

Similarly, when a teacher draws a diagram on the board, students dutifully copy it into their notes, but when they look over their notes before the test, they cannot remember what the diagram was about. Write a caption or title for all diagrams. Label them. Describe them. Don't just copy down a pretty picture that will not mean much to you a few weeks from now.

Figure 9.6   Separate the title or topic heading from the notes with a
blank line. Start a new idea on a new line. Your goal is to
make your notes as easy to read as possible.

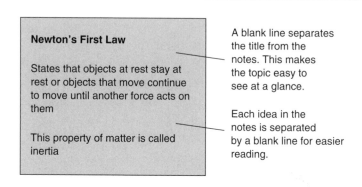

Newton's First Law

States that objects at rest stay at
rest or objects that move continue
to move until another force acts on
them

This property of matter is called
inertia

A blank line separates
the title from the
notes. This makes
the topic easy to
see at a glance.

Each idea in the
notes is separated
by a blank line for easier
reading.

Often, teachers write down only key ideas or words on the
board, but they say a lot more. Students sometimes fall into
the trap of writing down what was written, but they do not
record any of the other important information being said. You
should record not only what the teacher has written but also
what he or she says. You do not want to copy down only a
word and then find, a few weeks later when you turn to your
notes to study for the test, that you are unable to remember
anything about that term.

It is a good idea to take notes only on the right side of the
page. This permits you to write additional notes, thoughts,
and comments on the left side.

Finally, it can be helpful to sit next to a friend. You may be
able to share information as you take notes, and sometimes
you may even e-mail your notes to each other. This is a very
effective use of peer collaboration.

10

Note-Taking Shortcuts

Dear Teacher,

    I have trouble taking notes fast enough to keep up with the teacher. Are there any shortcuts I could use?

Sincerely,

Less Is More

Dear Less,

Try using symbols. There are many symbols and abbreviations that are faster to write than the words themselves. Figure 10.1 lists some of them. I am sure you can find others.

You can also make your own abbreviations. For example, if you are studying the Declaration of Independence, you might write out the whole title the first time, followed by the abbreviation (DI) you will use from then on. In other words, you would write "Declaration of Independence (DI)" the first time, and then just DI each time thereafter.

Get in the habit of coding your notes. I suggest that you use those codes shown in Figure 10.2.

Figure 10.3 shows what your notes might look like when you use shortcuts and codes.

Taking notes is a very difficult skill to learn because it involves listening, thinking, summarizing, and writing—all at the same time. Our brains can focus on only one thought at a time. You are thinking about what you are writing down, but the teacher has moved forward and has already started talking about something new. You can only pay attention to writing down your notes *or* to what the teacher is saying. Your brain has

Figure 10.1   Common symbols that can speed up the rate at which you take notes.

=	is, becomes, equals, same
e.g.	for example, such as
i.e.	that is, what I mean is, in other words
>	greater than
<	less than
/	or, per
@	at
w/	with
w/o	without
+	and
diff	difference, differing, differentiate
dev	develop, development, developing

Figure 10.2 Typical codes to use in your notes.

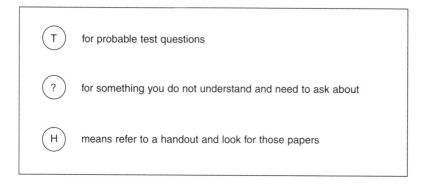

(T) for probable test questions

(?) for something you do not understand and need to ask about

(H) means refer to a handout and look for those papers

Figure 10.3 Example of notes recorded on the Cornell method form, using shortcuts and codes.

(T)

inertia

examples

(?)

Newton's first law of motion = inertia

What is the 1st law? — see yesterday's notes

Inertia is the tendency of an object to remain at rest or to continue moving until it is acted upon by another force.

e.g., book on table stays on table until pushed

e.g., skater continues gliding in same direction @ same speed until friction slows her down

i.e., all objects have inertia

What is net force for an object at rest?

Introduction to Inertia/ Newton's First Law

tendency of an object to keep doing what it is doing

to make a choice: do I stop writing and listen, thereby missing some of the notes, or do I continue to write and miss something important? Become a partner with the teacher. Ask the teacher to repeat what he or she said. If the teacher moves on and starts to say something new while you are still writing notes about the previous sentence, you should raise your hand and ask the teacher to wait a moment. No one knows you are having trouble keeping up but you, so sending that signal helps your teacher. You will find most teachers will be quite accommodating, especially in the lower grade levels, when you ask them to repeat something. The art of note taking takes years to develop, and teachers are usually quite sensitive to that and want to help.

For the same reason, it is difficult to take notes if something is going on in class that distracts you. You need to give the process of note taking your focused attention. You may find this to be hard to do at first, but we *can* learn to ignore distractions (Levine, 2002). This is not an easy skill to master, but practice, self-awareness, and determination will really help. The first step is to recognize what distracts you. Is it a friend sitting next to you with whom you talk? If so, then choose a different seat. If you think your friend will be hurt, you should explain that you are getting distracted, that you need to improve your school work, and that you don't want either you or your friend to be caught talking.

If your mind wanders, make a note as soon as you check back in. Record when you lost focus and how long your mind was wandering. Keep a list of these times. You want to become much more aware of things that distract you, and you want to reduce your periods of unfocused time in both number and duration. Do you fiddle with things? Are your hands in constant motion? Try playing with only one item (for example, quietly twirl a pencil or gently tap the desk, but remember: you do not want to distract the person sitting next to you). If you sit toward the back of the classroom and are distracted by seeing what everyone is doing in front of you, take a seat in the front row. If your teacher assigns seats, explain your problem and ask the teacher to move you. Learn to advocate for yourself! If you sit next to a friend who is aware of your problem and who wants to help, ask that person to give you a nudge whenever you seem to be drifting off.

Now here is the hard part. You need to work with a coach in order to overcome your distractibility. You should both talk every day. Share your list with your coach. I'll be honest: distractibility is a difficult problem for some students, and you will have to work really hard to overcome it. People who are easily distracted often suffer from a deep sense of embarrassment and guilt (Hallowell & Ratey, 1994). I want you to praise yourself every chance you get, so if you have a day in which you are less distracted, you should celebrate and your coach should praise you. Whatever you do, do not use your distractibility as an excuse. Remember: do not project the problem onto others, such as your teacher. Take full responsibility for your behaviors and for improving them.

11

Taping a Class

Dear Teacher,

   Taking notes is difficult for me. Should I use a tape recorder in class?

Sincerely,

Fast Forward

Dear Fast,

Generally, taping classes is not a good idea. It is very time consuming. For every minute spent in class, you will have to spend the same amount of time listening to the tape. If you tape five 50-minute classes during the day, you will have to spend over four hours at night just listening to your classes for a second time! No one has that much free time.

The idea of recording classes might be appealing, but it causes problems for students. Because you think you are getting everything down, you run the very real risk of focusing less and less in class. As a result, you will miss some of the points the teacher made. And just because you have the information on tape does not mean you know it or understand it. You want the information to be in your head. Also, because you are not really listening, you won't know if something the teacher said confuses you until it is too late—that is, when you listen to the tape at home and the teacher is not there.

You may also find the quality of the tape is so poor that you miss things that were said. Some tape recorders have microphones that pick up too much, and the background noise that you record may prevent you from hearing what the teacher and the students said. Similarly, you may miss what some people said because the tape recorder could not pick up their voices if they sat far away.

Tape recorders have another limitation that we usually do not think about until it is too late. Taped classes will not help you review for tests. You really need to look at notes that are well formatted on paper, that highlight the main points and include added detail to help you understand the concepts. This is where the Cornell method becomes such a powerful tool (read my letter in Chapter 9, Note-Taking Formats). By recording your notes on paper, you begin the process of making the teacher's information your own.

There is an additional problem you might face if you try to tape your class: your teacher might not like it. Some students tape their classes without their teachers' knowledge or permission, and that is discourteous.

It is important to remember that tape recording classes is not a substitute for taking notes. You should put your energy into developing your note-taking skills, no matter how hard that might be for you. You wrote that you are not very good at this skill. Okay, that simply means you will need to work a little harder at it. People who are not natural athletes have to do that when they learn a sport. It is the same with study skills like note taking. But you will get better at it the more you practice. That is what you need to do—practice!

PART III

Homework
Skills

Homework requires a student to be able to manage time effectively, to set up an environment that is conducive to concentration and learning, and to resist distractions. These expectations would be challenging for anyone, let alone a child.

In this section, I explore concerns and skills associated with nightly homework.

12

Recording Assignments

Dear Teacher,

I keep forgetting to write down my assignments. I call my friends and ask them, but I think they are beginning to be annoyed with me. Help!

Sincerely,

Assignmentless

Dear Assignmentless,

Your problem is not unusual, and we all forget to write down our assignments from time to time. The bad news is: you have an organizational problem; the good news is: it is easy to fix. After you read this answer, I think you should also read the next letter, in Chapter 13, just to be safe.

There are three ways to record assignments and none is perfect. The first is to carry an assignment book with you at all times. Record the assignment and when that work is due. If you use this technique, you will have to remember to carry the assignment book to each class, even though you change notebooks. The advantage is that all of your assignments will be recorded in one place.

Some students record their assignments in each class notebook. They keep some papers in the front of each notebook on which they write their assignments. The problem with this approach is that they will have to check each notebook as they pack up at the end of the day and decide which books they need to take home. Just because others use this system does not mean it will necessarily work for you. I do not recommend this system if you have difficulty with organization because it will be hard to remember to look at each notebook.

The third technique assumes you use a laptop in class. Format an assignment book and put it on your desktop, where you can see it every time you open your laptop.

In each case, record your assignment as soon as it is given in class. If your teacher writes the assignments on the board, get in the habit of writing them down as soon as you walk in the classroom. If the assignment is given on e-mail or on the Web, get in the habit of checking it as soon as you walk in the door, and copy it to your assignment file. If the teacher gives out the assignments during class, write them down in the proper location right away.

Now for the important part: check the assignment book or computer file when class is over, *before* you leave the room, to be sure you wrote down the assignment. In this way, you will have all of your assignments for all of your subjects in the same place each day. Pretty soon, your friends will start calling *you*!

Find yourself a coach to help you. Explain your problem and how you intend to overcome it. Show your assignment-recording system to your coach each evening. You might both decide that if you forget to write down an assignment, you should lose a small privilege. More important, you should receive a reward each time you record every assignment. I always like the rewards to be larger than the punishments!

13
Misplaced Homework

Dear Teacher,

I tell my teacher I do my homework, but when it comes time to turn it in, I can't find it. My grade suffers, and I think my teacher does not believe me. Do you have any suggestions?

Sincerely,

Lost

Dear Lost,

Because of the way you phrased your letter, I'm guessing that perhaps you don't always do your homework, or that sometimes you forget to do it or run out of time and don't do it completely. Perhaps you don't bring home the materials you need in order to do it. I also suspect when you get to school, you sometimes discover you have left your homework at home. I even would not be surprised if you had said that when the teacher announces the homework assignment, you are no longer listening. You are concentrating more on where you have to go next and on packing up. But no matter how you slice it, you have an organizational problem. Luckily, organizational skills can be improved.

Do you write down your homework assignments in the same place each day? This is important (read my previous letter). If you write them down in different places, you will have to hunt around for them, and you will probably miss one or two of them. When you are packing up at the end of the day to go home, you need to look at your assignments so you know what to bring home.

When you finish a homework assignment, check it off on the assignment sheet. This lets you know you have done the work. As you do your homework, you get to see how much you have accomplished and how much remains. Keeping track of your progress is a valuable organizational skill.

Buy a plastic folder that seals shut, and keep it in the front of your notebook. When you finish your homework paper or worksheet, immediately put it in the folder. Now you will always know where to look for your homework!

At the end of the evening, as you put away all your books, check your assignment sheet one last time to be sure you did everything, and then look in each folder to be sure you put the homework papers in them. It never hurts to double-check and to reinforce the new organizational skills you are trying to learn.

Sometimes I recommend that a student ask each teacher, "Am I caught up?" at the end of every week. This is a safety check to be sure you did not forget to turn in a paper. It also sends a signal to the teacher that you are trying to improve.

Finally, share your problem and what you are trying to do about it with a coach. Initially, your coach might want to check your assignments sheets and homework folders each night. Later, as you begin to get used to this new system, maybe all you will have to do is to check in with your coach.

This kind of organizational skill takes a while to learn. You will need an adult's involvement, and you will need to be patient and keep at it.

14

Why Even Do Homework?

Dear Teacher,

Why do I have to do homework? What does it do for me? I'd rather go out and play.

Sincerely,

Wanna Have Fun

Dear Wanna,

Of course you would rather go out and have a good time. That is a normal desire, and it is a perfect example of the *pleasure-pain principle* (*Psychological Self-Help Tools*, n.d.). Simply put, this principle says that your brain would prefer to avoid anything that is painful and, instead, do things that give it pleasure. Let's face it: studying is hard work, and work can be painful. When you do your homework, your brain has to focus and think and jump through all sorts of mental hoops, and that is just not fun. Talking and playing with friends is much less work. Furthermore, these activities involve a much lower level of thinking, or what we call cognitive functioning, so playing is easier for your brain. But homework is important, and it is assigned for many valid reasons.

Homework helps you do better in school and in life. By doing homework, you reinforce the skills you have only begun to learn in class. The more effective attention that you give to your homework, the better you will do in school. Homework serves to introduce new topics before they are taught in class and revisits material already explored. The more times students are exposed to material, the more likely they are to remember it, so homework strengthens your memory. This strengthening process is called *consolidation* (De Fina, 2003). Homework is assigned because it expands on material beyond what can be taught in class. It lets you apply what you are learning to new situations. Research studies have found that students who do homework do better in class (Cooper, 1994), so doing homework can lead to higher grades. It increases the retention of factual knowledge and leads to a better understanding of concepts. Sometimes teachers take homework questions and put them on tests or quizzes. If you don't do your homework, your chances of doing well on those questions are diminished. Homework even increases our curiosity.

Homework also teaches organizational skills and responsibility. These are important life skills. Before you leave the classroom, you have to be sure you wrote down the assignment. Before you leave school, you have to check you have all the books and papers you will need to do that assignment. You have to schedule your time at home so you will be able to do this work. By doing the assigned work, you learn how to follow directions. You develop skills needed to become an independent learner. By doing homework, you learn how to be accountable to yourself. Homework teaches *autonomy*, or independence; it teaches you how to take charge of your own life. It teaches you how to persevere; when faced with a challenge, you learn how to stick with the problem until you solve it. Homework increases your self-reliance; when you do your homework correctly, you feel empowered. It teaches self-motivation. Your teachers or parents do not follow you around all day to remind you to study; you need to do that yourself. If you learn these skills now, you will be ahead of the group.

So, Wanna, you have a decision to make. You can continue to play and ignore your academic responsibilities, or you can decide to reach a compromise: accept that your school work must come first, complete your studies, and play at other times. I think you will find you can do both, and if you meet your school obligations, I suspect you will be very pleased by the results.

15

Location, Location, Location— What Is a Good Study Environment?

Dear Teacher,

I do my homework in the kitchen while my mother prepares dinner. Is this a good idea?

Sincerely,

Well Fed

Dear Well Fed,

You need a quiet place in which to work, one that is free of distractions. That means no television, no telephone, and no noises of pots and pans as your mother makes dinner. You need a study environment that is well lit, has all the materials you will need, and in which you can spread out your texts and papers. The reason you need a quiet place is because you need to concentrate. It is much harder to do that when someone else is in the same room with you, doing things that you are bound to notice.

Since the 1950s, we have known the brain can focus with absolute clarity on only one thing at a time. This is due to something that has recently been called *inattentional blindness* (Cherry, 1953; Simons & Chabris, 1999; Wolfe, 2001a). To test this phenomenon, scientists put people on two teams. The teams were then told to pass a basketball back and forth while moving around and to count the number of times their teammates caught the ball. Partway through the experiment, a man dressed in a gorilla suit walked into the room, paused in the middle, and then left. When asked later, 50% of the people said they never saw the gorilla. They were focusing on their task so completely that their brains were unable to take in any other information. This is like the parent who is talking on the phone when a child approaches and asks a question. The parent stops and says, "Not now, honey. I'm on the phone." The parent can either listen to the person on the phone or to the child, but not both.

That is exactly like you. You can either concentrate on your homework or you can pretend to do it while also being aware of your mother as she cooks. Find a more appropriate location in which to do your work, one that is more appropriate to the task you are trying to accomplish (read the next letter to learn how to set up a good study environment).

16

Sit on the Floor or at My Desk? Setting Up an Effective Study Environment

Dear Teacher,

I don't like to work at my desk. I prefer to study while sitting on the floor. My parents say I should sit in a chair and work at my desk. When I do work at my desk, my mother complains that it is messy and too distracting, but it doesn't bother me. Who is right?

Sincerely,

Really Floored

Dear Really,

When it comes to working at your desk or sitting on the floor, I think both you *and* your parents are right. We used to tell students they should sit up straight in a chair and always work at a desk. I have learned, however, that some students really can study certain subjects effectively while sitting on the floor. For example, some people like to read while sitting somewhere other than at their desk. Whenever you have to write, however, you should sit at a desk. Writing should always be done on a flat, smooth surface. Some students work at their desk as they prepare study cards and memorize the material, but when they recite what they have learned, they find they must stand up and pace back and forth. So different people study in the environment that works the best for them.

There is one place no one should study, and that is lying down on the bed (or anywhere else). After a long day at school, you are tired. When you lie down, you send a signal to your brain that you should relax and prepare to fall asleep. If you read a book while you are lying down, your concentration drops markedly. You won't have much success if you try to study this way.

I think your mother has a point about your messy desk. Not only do you need to work in a quiet place where you can concentrate, you also need a clean space, one that has been properly set up for the job you are about to do.

Prepare a large workspace for yourself. You want enough room to spread out all of your papers and books, and you want to remove anything that could be particularly distracting. A place where you study and do nothing else is best. After a while, you will begin to associate that space with study, and concentrating and focusing will become easier for you.

Have a solid, flat surface for writing, whether you are doing your math homework, writing a paper, or preparing graphic organizers. Have all of the supplies you will need—pencils, rulers, index cards, etc.—in a place that is out of the way but easy to reach. Have a clock that is visible; you will have to pace yourself and be sure you are keeping to your schedule. You will need good lighting—neither too bright nor too dim. Your chair should be comfortable and give you enough support so you do not become tired from sitting. Eliminate all distractions, including television, loud music, computers, and telephones. Be sure to wear your glasses, if you need them for reading. The area should be well ventilated. A stuffy room that builds up carbon dioxide causes a loss in concentration. The temperature should be comfortable—neither too warm nor too cold.

Are you distracted by other noises in the house? Some students go to the hardware store and buy inexpensive ear protectors; others go to the pharmacy and buy earplugs that muffle and block outside noises so they can study better.

Periodically clean your workspace. When you do, you are making the statement to yourself that "this is the place I associate with studying, and that is important to me." Realize, however, that setting up a workspace and cleaning it can distract you from doing your homework. You should not organize this area during the time when you are supposed to be studying.

Eventually, you will become so used to studying in a clean and proper work environment that you will just work there out of habit and preference.

17

Background Music and Homework

Dear Teacher,

I have been told I should study in a quiet room. But I find I can concentrate better if I have some background music. Am I doing the right thing?

Sincerely,

Heavenly Sounds

Dear Heavenly,

Thirty years ago, we were told we had to have absolute quiet in order to study effectively. Someone even tested my reading rate to drive home the message. First, I read a passage in a quiet room and then I read another, similar passage when the radio was blaring. My reading rate was much faster in the quiet room. I was really not impressed by this demonstration. Who studies in a room with music so loud you would have to yell at the person next to you just to be heard? When I am doing work that does not require absolute concentration—for example, drawing a graph—I often have some classical music softly playing in the background (certainly not the kind of music that was played during that test).

There can be benefits from playing music. It sets a certain rhythm. I know of one boy who could not do his math homework in study hall. He was fidgety and could not concentrate. He was so restless he disturbed other students. He told his teacher he could not work in such a quiet room. Luckily, that teacher was willing to try something unusual. She said he could bring his portable CD player to study hall as long as it had earphones and did not disturb anyone else. They would see if it helped. The boy was instantly transformed. He sat at his desk for the entire period. He not only did his math, but some of his other homework, too. Music can act like white noise, drowning out distracting noises that happen in your house. So I am not opposed to having some music playing softly in the background.

If you play music, there are problems you have to guard against. If you play the music too loudly, it will interfere with your studies. If you find yourself concentrating on the music, perhaps singing along with it, you need to turn down the volume or find a different kind of music. When you start to memorize material, you will probably have to turn off the music because you need to focus only on the memorization process. You need to learn to self-monitor if you do play music, and you need to be prepared to turn it off if it gets in the way of your studying.

I hope you do not play the television while you study. TV is distracting and severely reduces your ability to focus on your work. Similarly, you should not leave the computer on so you can hear when someone wants to engage you in a chat. Each time you hear the chime, you will be distracted. To say this differently, you won't be able to study as effectively and efficiently as I am sure you would like.

18
Wandering Focus

Dear Teacher,

My mind wanders when I study. What can I do?

Sincerely,

Wanderful

Dear Wanderful,

We all suffer from distraction. The hard part is to become aware when it happens and to get back on track.

You need to discuss this problem with your coach and work as a team to overcome it. Start by talking with your coach daily: Identify when your mind wanders. What do you do when it wanders? How long do you remain in your wandering state? Talking about and identifying the parts of a problem make up the first step in overcoming it.

Once you have acknowledged you are easily distracted, you and your coach need to look for solutions. Do you start doing something else when your mind begins to wander? Schedule that activity for another time. Do you suddenly remember that you need to do something? Write it down on a piece of paper to do later and go back to work. Do you begin to think about that magazine that is on the floor near your desk? Move the magazine so it is out of sight. *Subvocalize* as you study, if necessary, to bring your mind back on task and to keep it there. For example, if you are reading a text, read it quietly out loud so that you hear the words and are forced to concentrate on the material. Sit up straight. You might even have to rework your schedule. Turn to something easier and come back to this assignment a bit later.

There is a neat trick that works for some students. When you find your mind is wandering, stand up. Turn around so that you are facing away from your desk and books. Don't walk away or leave the room, but do some simple stretching exercises for about half a minute. Turn back to your desk, sit down, and resume your work.

You turn away from your work area just to help make the point to yourself that you are not associating your loss of focus and this stretching exercise with study. Stretching speeds up the circulation a bit, bringing more oxygen to the brain, which it needs in order to be active. When you return to your work, you will be refreshed and better able to concentrate on the task at hand.

I have watched students stretch during long tests and exams. They don't get up from their desks, of course, but they quietly stretch their arms and legs, move their hands and wriggle their fingers, and roll their heads on their shoulders. When they do this, they relax muscles that might be getting tense and they improve the circulation to their brains. This helps them to keep their focus. Try it!

Distraction is a difficult problem to overcome, but with help and determination, you can do it. You seem to have the desire to improve, and that is a large part of the battle that each of us experiences. Good luck!

19

Pressure Versus Stress

Dear Teacher,

I work better under pressure. Doesn't everyone? So I wait until the last minute before I begin my work.

Sincerely,

Craves Pressure

Dear Craves,

There is a difference between pressure and stress (Sapolsky, 2003; Sprenger, 1999). Stress is more extreme and causes the release of chemicals in your brain that interfere with everything from your ability to concentrate to your ability to ward off colds. When you study in a stressful environment, the chances are the quality of learning is poor, and what is learned will be quickly forgotten—perhaps even before you take the test! Unlike stress, pressure can be motivating; you seem to thrive on it.

In and of itself, pressure can be good, but waiting until the last minute may not be the wisest way to approach your work. Sooner or later, this strategy will backfire. What will you do if you wait until the last minute and then discover that your project requires more time? What will you do if you set aside what you had thought would be enough time to accomplish this task, only to have another teacher assign a test for the same day? What will you do if you put the work aside until the last minute and then get sick and find you do not have enough energy to finish the job?

Furthermore, waiting until the last minute and studying the night before the test does not produce the highest grades. If you spread out your work over two or more days, you will actually retain more information (read my letter in Chapter 37, Forgetting and Cramming). Creating an artificial pressure by waiting until the last minute is not a formula for success.

I suggest you find a new source of pressure. Instead of waiting until the last minute and using time to create a sense of pressure, try substituting the goal of excellence. Let the pressure come from within yourself. Start your work earlier and try to do the best possible job on it that you can. Do not accept anything less than your absolute best. That kind of pressure will benefit you the most in the long run.

20

Homework Schedules

Dear Teacher,

I know I should write a homework schedule for myself, but I don't know how to do it.

Sincerely,

Hoping for Ideas

Dear Hoping,

Homework schedules are wonderful tools. They make you more self-aware and help you use your time more effectively. They help keep you on task. They also help you to use your time efficiently.

The trick is to create a schedule that establishes a routine and yet can be somewhat flexible. For example, imagine you usually finish your math homework in 20 minutes, so you always start with that. Sometimes, however, you might be given a very challenging problem and you will need an extra 10 minutes to solve it. Your schedule cannot be so rigid that you always stop after 20 minutes, regardless of your real need. You have to extend the math study time and take the 10 minutes from somewhere else (perhaps your parents will excuse you from washing the dishes!). Similarly, imagine you have a very easy assignment and finish early. You would not just sit at your desk until you reached the time when you should begin your next assignment. Be intelligently adaptable.

Having advised you to be flexible, I have to add that there is an exception. Some teachers or schools publish rules and guidelines about how long homework should take. For example, you might be told that each teacher should assign no more than 30 minutes of homework per night. If you find a particular assignment is taking far too long, you should stop doing it and turn to your other assignments. You can return to this overly long assignment if time permits. You should tell your teacher this was an exceptionally long assignment and agree upon how the work will be completed. Every now and then, a teacher misjudges how long an assignment will take, and everyone takes longer than expected to complete the work. When that happens, I would hope that your teacher would be reasonable and make the appropriate adjustments to your next assignment so that you might have the time to complete it. Please note that I am not talking about an assignment that took a few extra minutes. I am also not thinking of an assignment that took a long time because you work very slowly or because you kept getting distracted; those are different problems that you, not the teacher, need to address. When you go to school the next day, talk to your friends. You will quickly discover if many of them spent a long time completing the assignment or if you need to meet with your teacher to learn how you should approach your work in that class.

Most students need to create a schedule at one time or another. Some students have poor time-management skills and need to learn and use consistently the structure and discipline that a schedule provides. These students will need to write a schedule every night. Other students find they begin to need a schedule only when their workload increases beyond a certain level, perhaps toward the end of the marking period and around exam time. If you need help from a schedule, keep writing one until managing your time effectively becomes a habit.

When you write a schedule, you need to include everything. Write down when you leave school, what you do on the way home, what time you get home, how long you give yourself to raid the kitchen before you settle down, and how long a break you allow yourself between subjects. You also need to take into account long-term projects and upcoming tests and quizzes.

First write a schedule for tonight. It should be pretty accurate. You probably won't have to change it very much. Write another schedule for tomorrow and one for the next night. These will be less accurate. You will have to update them as the time gets closer and you gain a more accurate picture of your assignments. Then consider what you will be doing for the rest of the week. Do not forget to give yourself time to relax over the weekend—play time is vital. You need to be aware of upcoming events that might impinge on your study time. Do your parents expect you to go to a family gathering? Will your soccer practice run longer than usual? The reason you need to create a schedule that looks a few days into the future is so you can plan your work. You may need two days, for example, to study for a test, and you may have to start tonight. You may have a long-term project, and you will need to spend some time on it each night.

Figure 20.1   A typical study schedule.

3:30	leave school
4:00	shop for a new squash racket
5:00	arrive home
5:00–5:15	free time/snack
5:15–5:45	math
5:45–5:50	break
5:50–6:20	English
6:20–6:25	break
6:25–6:40	science
6:40–6:46	break
6:46–7:00	current events
7:00–7:30	dinner
7:30–7:55	history
7:55–8:08	break
8:08–8:35	Spanish
8:35–9:00	call friends
9:00–9:30	practice violin
9:45	get ready for bed, read, lights out

Examine the evening study schedule in Figure 20.1. Let's say this is the first schedule you wrote up for yourself.

Notice you gave yourself some time at the beginning of the evening to read your mail, grab a snack, change out of school clothes, or whatever. You also gave yourself a short break between each period of work in which you got up from your desk and did something physical. This does not mean that you put down your English reading assignment and started to read a magazine article. You know your brain needs a total change of pace. Perhaps you decided to go downstairs and play with the dog or to get up from your desk, swinging your arms back and forth, and throw your dirty clothes in the hamper.

Breaks are important. Scientists have found that our brains still learn while we are on a break (Foster & Wilson, 2006). We may not be aware of it, but our brain is processing information at a subconscious level. Movement is also important. It increases blood flow to the brain, giving it more oxygen and removing the toxic waste products of the metabolism of glucose, the sugar that powers the brain.

You took a long break at dinner. It takes a few minutes for your brain to begin to refocus and concentrate after you return to your desk. You know that, so you gave yourself a little extra time at 7:30. History didn't take as long as you had thought it would when you wrote this schedule. You actually finished at 7:51. You rewarded yourself by allowing yourself four minutes to go online. That is not a lot of time, but all you wanted to do was to check to see if a friend had responded to your e-mail. Remember, a schedule is a tool. You need to be able to make intelligent changes to it as you go along. On some nights, you might have to assign a longer period of time to a subject because you have to write a paper. Some courses might require a much shorter amount of time because all you need to do is review your notes. You want to make the schedule accurately reflect the amount of time you require to complete each assignment.

Why did you decide to study math first and Spanish last? Generally, you should study the hardest subjects earlier in the evening when your brain is most alert and study the easier subjects later, when your brain is getting tired. You decided, however, to put math first because all you had to do was prac- tice problems. You decided this would be a warm-up exercise for your brain. It would help you to begin to concentrate, something you will really need to do when you begin your English because that homework involves diagramming sen- tences, and grammar is hard for you. You put science next because you are studying a topic that really does not interest you. You know if you study it later, you will miss too many key points. You put Spanish last because you love that subject. It is easy for you, and you wanted to have something fun to look forward to. If you had had to prepare for a quiz in Spanish, you would have moved it to a much earlier slot. You want to mem- orize material when you are relatively fresh. You would have then done other work and returned to the Spanish later in the evening to reinforce what you had memorized and so you could test yourself to see if you still remembered the material.

Don't throw your schedules away when those days have passed. Keep them in a folder or a notebook. By keeping them, you are telling yourself they are important to you. Also, you will be able to refer to them in order to determine the average time you spend on each subject. This information can be very helpful as you try to create a meaningful schedule.

Share your schedule with your parents. You need to work as a team when you plan afterschool or weekend activities. Your parents need to be aware of your academic responsibilities when they plan family outings. Also, you are much more likely to keep to your schedule if you include a parent who will act as a coach. Each evening, talk about how you are managing your time. Are you finding it easier to plan? Are you beginning to get a sense of how long things take you? Are you getting everything done? Are you wasting less time? Be patient; learning how to use schedules takes some time.

How much time should you spend creating your schedule? I do not think you should spend more than about three minutes on a schedule—five if you have to check with your parents about anything they had planned for you that you might not have known about. A schedule is just a tool and you will adjust it as you go along, so don't spend too much time making it look pretty.

Do not fall into the trap of thinking that making a schedule is doing your homework. It is not. It is just a preparatory activity. You do not want to waste time trying to create the perfect schedule or one that looks really nice. It is going to be marked up and changed anyway. Spend your precious study time on things that are really important, like homework.

A schedule gets you used to putting the same time aside each night to do your homework. It helps you see whether you have time to chat on the phone with your friends. It helps you learn how to organize your time. It gives you concrete evidence to show your parents when you want to impress them with how responsible you are trying to be! It also gives you something to share with your teachers or advisor when they ask you if you are spending enough time on your homework. A schedule helps you learn how to manage your time. This is an important life skill.

21

Ready, Set . . . Don't Start— Procrastination

Dear Teacher,

I don't mind studying, once I get started. I just have trouble starting. I tend to put things off until the last minute. Maybe I'm just not motivated. Do you have any suggestions?

Sincerely,

Putting It Off

Dear Putting,

I think you would like to get started; you just do not know how. Part of your problem has to do with the pleasure-pain principle (read my letter in Chapter 14, Why Even Do Homework?). I suspect, however, that for the most part, you are just procrastinating—you are avoiding your work. Sometimes the most difficult challenge we face is just getting started. Each of us procrastinates from time to time, but when we do it more often than not, we have a problem.

The first step in overcoming this problem is simply to acknowledge that you are procrastinating. Then step back and look at yourself. What are you doing when you are avoiding your work? To ask this a bit differently, what do you do instead of your work? Once you begin to recognize when you are procrastinating and that you are using the same avoidance behaviors repeatedly, you can change.

When you do sit down to do your homework, try starting with an easy or small assignment for the first few weeks. You will probably find it easier to keep going once you start. After you become used to sitting down and working, you can think about creating a more appropriate homework schedule (read my letter in Chapter 20, Homework Schedules).

Plan appropriate rewards for yourself each time you complete a part of your work. Procrastination has as much to do with your attitude as anything else. Positive reinforcement (rewards) when you do the right thing really helps you to do away with bad habits as you try to develop new ones. Improving study skills has a lot to do with replacing old, detrimental habits with new, more effective habits.

Finally, talk with your coach about your tendency to procrastinate and the progress you are making as you try to conquer this behavior. Sharing a problem with someone else helps us to eliminate it.

22

Giving Too Much Help to Friends

Dear Teacher,

   My friends call me all the time for help on their homework. I like to help, but it takes a lot of time. I do not want to lose my friends. What can I do?

Sincerely,

Reluctant Homework Buddy

Dear Reluctant,

Every time you are interrupted, you need at least two minutes to settle down and begin to concentrate again. When you are tired, you need even more time. That means every time you talk on the phone, you are adding to your study time by the length of the phone call plus two or more minutes. It is wonderful to help others, but your friends are not being fair to you. They are not thinking of your needs, only their own.

Talk with your friends and tell them everyone needs to agree not to call until a certain time. That may be after you have finished all of your homework or at a certain time when you know you need to take a 10-minute break. Explain that while one phone call may last only five minutes, the time really adds up when you have many calls in one evening. Of course, they will not like being told they cannot call whenever they want. You have been a free source of help and, frankly, have been doing their work for them. But they are your friends. They like you. They might complain when you tell them not to call you at certain times, but they are just testing you; they won't leave you, despite what you might fear. And if they do, they are not your friends. Don't cave in to their pressure.

Talk with your parents about your plan (They will think you are being very mature and responsible!), and ask them for their help. Ask them to answer the phone and to explain that you are studying and unavailable. Ask them to take a message and say you will call back at the hour you agreed to make your calls. If you own a cell phone, turn it off while you are studying, after leaving a message saying that you will return the call at a certain time.

But remember, fair is fair. If your friends cannot call you, you cannot call them in the middle of their study time when you have a homework question.

23

Too Much Parental Help

Dear Teacher,

My mother likes to check my homework. She makes corrections. She helps me write my papers. Is this a good idea?

Sincerely,

Dependent

Dear Dependent,

The fact that you wrote this letter suggests you already know the answer. There is a difference between a parent who helps a child with a specific problem and one who does the work *for* the child. The answer is no, it is not a good idea.

It is perfectly normal for parents of children in grades K–3 to check that their child is doing homework each day and to be available for help. In grades 4–6, parents withdraw a little bit. But by the seventh grade, parents should let students work independently, with only occasional exceptions. Sometimes parents can be confused about the role they should play. There is a difference between being a coach and being intrusive. The former is supportive while the latter takes away the student's right to make mistakes and experience true achievement.

You need to have a talk with your mother. You need to remind her that you are the person being graded by your teachers, not her. To claim someone else's work as your own is dishonest. Often, students who receive inappropriate amounts of help at home and earn high grades on homework find their scores on in-class work and tests are much lower. Of course there is a disparity in grades. Unlike the test, the homework that was turned in does not accurately reflect the student's knowledge and skills. It was not written in the language of the student. Your teacher, who might not say anything, is sure to have noticed the differences in your grades and your writing style. At the very least, your teacher will be suspicious and may alert other teachers; at worst, you may even be accused of plagiarism—turning in work that was written by someone else. You do not want that to happen. Your reputation is too important. Your greatest asset is the trust that other people have in you. Once it is lost, that trust is very hard to regain. Don't jeopardize it.

It is one thing to go to a parent when you are stuck on a problem and need a little guidance, but it is another thing entirely when that parent does the work for you. Often, the parent intrudes, thinking high grades are all that are important, no matter how they are obtained. This misses the real point, however. The parent who does the work takes away the learning opportunity from the child. When the work has already been done, there is nothing left to be learned. This is not helping. It is actually holding the child back. If the child is not given a chance to learn, what will happen later on, when the parent is not present?

You are the person who needs to learn, and your mother needs to give you the opportunity to do so. Inevitably, you will make mistakes. You might even earn a failing grade or two. But you will learn from that failure. The truth is that we often learn more in life from our mistakes than from our successes, and we become stronger for them. You must be given the freedom to learn and to grow—on your own.

But if your mother stops helping you, you won't earn those high grades anymore, you say. Well, you were never the person who truly earned those high grades anyway, were you? Who knows what grades you will be capable of earning once you learn to stand on your own two feet? It is time for you to take ownership of this part of your life.

24

Brief Nightly Review of Notes

Dear Teacher,

   Why do I have to study notes at night?

Sincerely,

Trying to Avoid Work

Dear Trying,

Reviewing your notes each night is important because we quickly forget what happened in class. Forgetting is normal. In fact, most of us will forget 70%–90% of the detail that we hear in class within 24 hours (Carraway, 2003; Sousa, 2001). The point is, we do not retain very much just by sitting in a class and listening to the teacher. We follow along and we understand, but we do not move much of that information into our long-term, or permanent, memory. To do that, we need to learn to read over our notes when we do our homework at night.

Actually, even before you go home, before you review your notes, there is a strategy you can use to help stabilize some of your memory of what you learned in class. When you leave the classroom, as you walk to the next class with a friend, talk about one or two things that were taught in the class. Researchers have found that the simple act of discussion helps retain information (Schenck & Kosik, 2000). This conversation does not have to be deep and intellectual. Even a simple, "Wasn't that a cool film?" or "Did you understand what he meant when he talked about symbolism?" is enough to help fix some of the information in our brains. What a simple trick!

If you can, review your class notes each night in order to transfer even more information to your memory. Research has found that if you review a little every night, you are more likely to learn the material and will do better on tests (Wagner, 2002). You do not need to spend a lot of time on this—maybe three to five minutes—but you should look over your notes to be sure you still understand them. Even this short time spent looking at your notes reinforces your memory.

During this nightly review, fill in the Review column and the Summary section on your Cornell method notes (see my letter in Chapter 9, Note-Taking Formats). If you cannot review your notes every night, then you should develop the habit of looking at them every other night. When you go to school the next day, you will find that you will start up and be ready for class much more quickly than if you do no nightly review. Regular review of class notes also speeds up "relearning." Not surprisingly, researchers have discovered that if we learn something but do not use it, we forget it (Ratey, 2001). When we sit down to relearn it, such as when we study for a test, we learn it faster (De Fina, 2003). In other words, if you take a few minutes each night to look over what you have done in school during the day, you will find studying for tests will go more quickly.

I recommend you ask a parent to act as a coach for this skill. It is too easy to skip this nightly review, thinking you have too much homework. Nevertheless, it is a powerful technique that aids in developing understanding and memory, and I think a little adult assistance will help you to stick with the program until it becomes a habit.

25

How to Read Informational Texts

Dear Teacher,

Should I read a science textbook the same way I read a book for English?

Sincerely,

Bookworm

Dear Bookworm,

This is a really good question! When we were taught to read, we first learned to read letters, then words, and finally stories. We continue to practice our reading skills on "narrative literature," or fiction. I have not met anyone who was taught how to read a science book when in grade school. In fact, I have not met any student who was taught at any time that he or she should read science differently from any other kind of material. As a result, we tend to read everything the same way, whether it is a newspaper, a poem, a work of fiction, a play, a history text, or a science text. The material in a science text has a lot of information, which is different from a story that has to do with character, plot, and theme development.

We typically read fictional books in their entirety, from beginning to end, at a steady pace. In contrast, we typically read informational texts, like those in history or science, selectively. Some sentences are more important than others. We vary the speed at which we read as we move from section to section, reading some parts carefully and scanning others. We may even have to read some sections several times in order to absorb all the information and understand it.

There are several strategies you can use to improve your reading comprehension when you have to tackle an informational text. The first involves knowing *why* you are reading the assignment.

Imagine you are a doctor. You are in the medical library reading about a new treatment. You know why you are reading the scientific papers in front of you and you know what you are looking for. You skim over some sections, looking for what you want, and then you quickly zero in on the sections that tell you what you need to learn. You slow down and read those parts very carefully. One paragraph is particularly difficult, so you read it twice. This is what you do if you know what is important as you read. You may breeze through the introductory paragraphs and then slow down when you reach the heart of the material. But this is not what most students do.

In school, unlike that doctor, you might not really know why you are reading a particular assignment. Usually, students read a text because they have been told to do so. They probably do not know why the topic is important; they just read it, hoping they'll find out as they go along. You do not have to fall into this trap, however. You can find out why you are reading the assignment.

Take about 30 to 45 seconds to find out what you are about to read. Flip through the assignment. Look at the headings. Glance at some of the key words. Look at the pictures. Most important, if there are questions at the end of the reading assignment or at the end of the chapter, read them. These questions suggest what the author thought was important. When possible, rephrase the questions, putting them into your own words. Some people call this activity "prereading."

You now have a sense of what you are about to read. As you performed this prereading exercise, you may have noticed some key words, and you will be looking for them as you read. Most important, you read some questions, and you will be looking for the answers.

Scientists did a study in which they asked students to read a simple, elementary-level textbook. They found that the students could remember, word for word, up to two sentences that they had just read. Then their memory faded (Schenck & Kosik, 2000). This happens because our working memory has limited space for great detail. If it becomes overloaded, it must drop information to make room for new, incoming information. Knowing this, I have to ask this question: why do textbook editors insist on putting questions at the end of a chapter? By the time you reach them, your brain has forgotten most or all of the answers. So by reading the questions first, you have primed your brain. You may forget a question or two (because working memory is limited in its capacity to retain information), but you will now read the assignment with greater attention. You know what to look for as you read. This is a very powerful technique. You will find that you will already have started to learn the material without even having to spend a lot of effort memorizing. But do not expect miracles. You won't remember everything, and you will still have to study before your tests. Nevertheless, this technique will help you.

Prereading tells you what to expect before you begin the assignment. A more subtle function of prereading is to help your brain to focus. It would far prefer to be doing something else. It needs to pay close attention to the task at hand. Prereading helps it to eliminate distractions. Practice prereading for at least two weeks, or about 10 reading assignments, whichever comes first. It may feel uncomfortable at first—new tasks or skills often seem awkward—but do not give up on it. It could make a big difference in your reading comprehension and how you retain information.

I also suggest that you learn to read with a pencil. I do not mean a highlighter, I really mean a pencil. I used to underline (because highlighters had not been invented yet) everything I knew was important and that I would have to study later on, when I had to prepare for the test. I remember I had a science text that was really meaty, and every line had some crucial or important information. I dutifully underlined as I read, thinking I was being so studious, underlining things I would have to study later. I looked at that text again a year or two after I had started teaching because I wanted to look up something, and I was really surprised. Every line was underlined for 34 pages! In most other sections, almost 90% of each page was underlined. I might as well have dipped the entire book in ink. Eventually, when I sat down and actually learned the material for the test, I must have had to reread all of those pages. What a waste of time that must have been! Students who paint their books with highlighters are said to be "highlighter happy." This is *not* what you want to do. Highlighting is not the same as learning.

Obviously, I used to think underlining was studying. It is not. It was just a way of saying to myself, "I know that is important," as I read the page. The same is true of highlighting. Both are really kind of mindless exercises that do not accomplish very much. You need to go a step or two further and use a strategy that can convert the book into a more useful study tool.

You need to use your pencil to *annotate* your text. This means you are going to mark the book using codes that will help you when you study for the test. First, find the main idea and put brackets around it. In some courses, the main idea is found in the topic sentence. In science, the main idea is probably not the topic sentence in a paragraph; you may find it in the title of the unit or the heading for the section. You may even have to read further in order to find the main idea.

Underline new vocabulary words or terms and the names of people you should know when they are first mentioned. Do *not* underline the definitions, just the term. Do not underline everything those people did. You do not want your textbook looking like mine! All you want to do is to draw your eye to the key parts of the assignment when you go back to study the material.

Put check marks in the margin by neat ideas or examples that might be helpful or that support and clarify a definition. I think of those things that I checked as being a little bit less important than any terms I may have underlined, but they are still valuable to know. You can even write a few words in the margin to explain why you put a check mark (for instance, "Example of inertia"). Draw a line from captions and material the editors may have written in the margins to the words and terms in the main text to which they refer. Finally, write notes to yourself in the margin. Those editors left a lot of white space in their books—use it! Make notes to yourself to connect what you are reading to a previous topic or to something said in class. Summarize a concept in a few words. Come up with a different example or use of the information. Is there something you just don't understand and should mark so you remember to ask the teacher the next day? Turn your text into the powerful study tool it was meant to be.

Some schools do not allow writing in books. If you are prohibited from marking up your texts, then use sticky notes to record key events, important facts, the sequence of events, or summarize important concepts. Similarly, when reading a work of fiction, write notes about character development, plot, or other important elements of the book, and attach them

Figure 25.1   The student who annotated this text page wrote a short summary in the white space after reading the assignment. What an effective study tool!

NEWTON'S LAWS OF MOTION

Have you ever ridden in a car, when the driver suddenly slammed on the brakes? What happened to you? Until 1687, no one truly understood motion. In that year, Sir Isaac Newton announced his three laws of motion. He was a well-known English mathematician and physicist who changed our understanding of the universe. His laws explained how objects move as they do.

The First Law of Motion

Newton's First Law of Motion consists of two parts. One part explains the behavior of stationary objects. It states that an object at rest remains at rest until an outside force acts upon it. Consider a ball that is sitting on the grass in the middle of a field. The ball will stay there until someone comes by and kicks it. By "outside," we mean that the force comes from something other than the ball.

The other part of the First Law describes what happens to moving objects. It states that an object in motion remains in motion until an outside force acts upon it. That kicked ball would continue to move across the field if the friction between the ball and ground did not slow it down. In this case, friction is the outside force. The First Law of Motion states that if you throw a ball, it will continue to move in a straight line until another force acts on it. The Earth's gravity, of course, is always acting on the ball, and it pulls the ball down toward the ground.

First Law: An object at rest will remain at rest, and an object in motion will continue to move in a straight line unless an outside force acts upon that object.

In other words, objects continue to do whatever it is they are doing until a force acts on them.

The tendency of an object to resist a change in motion is called inertia. The first law is all about inertia.

Figure 3.4 Have you ever wondered why you have to wear a seat belt? The doll sits on a cart that is rolling down a ramp. The cart stops when it hits the wall, but the doll has inertia and keeps moving forward. In an accident, seat belts protect us from the effect of our inertia.

to the appropriate pages. It is much easier to read these sticky notes than trying to reread an entire book!

Annotating a text accomplishes several things. First, you force your brain to pay closer attention while you read. This increases the amount you learn. Second, you convert your textbook into a much more effective study tool. You will find this to be very helpful when you get ready to study for your test. Finally, annotating texts forces you to alter your reading speed according to the difficulty of the material. This is exactly how you should read informational texts.

Here are a few other tips to help you understand and remember the information in the text. After reading a section in your textbook, try to recall the information contained in it. If there was something that you cannot remember or which did not make sense, reread that portion of the assignment. Writing short summaries of what you read can be a good idea, too. These will help you when it comes time to study for a test.

When you have finished reading the assignment, return to those questions that were at the end of the unit or the chapter and answer them. You will quickly find out whether you understood the reading or have to go back and read it again (or ask your teacher about it in class). By looking at those questions, you will also reinforce what you have learned, and that information will be more likely to stay in your brain.

26

Reading Rates

Dear Teacher,

Does everyone read at the same speed?

Sincerely,

Unrated

Dear Unrated,

People's reading rates differ, and they change according to what they are reading. The normal reading speed is 200 to 350 words per minute (Baker, 2005; "User Interface Design Update," 2000). But someone for whom reading is difficult might read the same material at speeds less than 200 words per minute. Also, we change our reading speed according to the difficulty of the material. For example, we slow way down when we read something that is hard to understand.

We tend to think at much faster rates than we read. (Years ago, I was told that we may think as fast as 3,500 words per minute!) One reason we think so quickly is because we do it in a shorthand kind of way. We don't think in complete sentences, and we think with a flash of emotion or an image that takes the place of words.

If our brains like to move at such lightning speeds and if reading is that slow, you can imagine the trouble you face while you read. You begin with interest, but your brain gets

Figure 26.1   How to calculate your average reading rate. You might try to determine your average reading speed for a novel, a history text, and a science text.

To calculate your average reading rate, set a kitchen timer for two minutes and begin reading when you press the START button. Stop when the bell rings and count the number of lines you read.
54 lines

Count the number of words on five lines of text and divide that number by 5 to obtain the average number of words per line.
62 words/5 lines = 12.4 words per line

Multiply the number of lines you read by the average number of words per line to obtain the total number of words that you read.
54 lines × 12.4 words/line = 669.6 words

Divide the number of words by two minutes to obtain the average number of words that you read in a minute.
$\dfrac{669.6 \text{ words}}{2 \text{ minutes}} = 335$ words per minute (rounded off)

bored by the slow pace and starts to think of other things. Your eyes may keep moving across the lines, but suddenly you find yourself at the bottom of the page and do not remember a single thing you have read. Your brain went off somewhere and has been working on something else.

Regardless of how fast you read, you need to find ways to keep your brain focused on what is on the page. (Read my letter in the previous chapter, How to Read Informational Texts, to discover how to annotate your text and help your brain pay attention as you read.)

27

Take Notes While Reading?

Dear Teacher,

Should I take notes while I read?

Sincerely,

Noteworthy

Dear Noteworthy,

I advise students to annotate their texts and to write in the margins (see my letter in Chapter 25, How to Read Informational Text). If you do this, you should not have to take notes as you read your textbook; that would be unnecessary work. Of course, if you are reading a book you do not own or which you cannot mark up, then you have to take notes.

If you must take notes, begin by recording the bibliographical information at the top of the note page: title of the book, author, publication dates, the pages you will read, and any other information your school might require. Use an outline format as you take notes on the reading material. Write down the main idea as the heading for your notes. Then skip a line and indent. Write down the important words and concepts from your reading, with their definitions. Skip a line (leaving enough white space makes it easier for your eyes to look over your notes later and provides space in which you can write additional thoughts) and indent again. Record any examples or supplementary information that may be helpful. When you get to the end of a section, write a brief summary of what you have read. Summaries should be short and in your own words. Summaries will help reinforce your understanding of what you have read.

If you are taking notes for a paper you will eventually write, be sure to mark your notes whenever you copy from the original source. Put quotation marks around the passage you copied word for word, and record the number of the page on which you found the information. If you write notes that are really just a paraphrase of the source material, at the end of that section of notes write *Paraphrased* and write down the page from which you took the material. You will need that information for your bibliography.

PART IV

Test Preparation and Test-Taking Skills

S tudying for tests is the hardest work students do, and so much depends on how well they do. Our goal is to give them command over the process.

Most students do not know the difference between working memory and long-term memory. Giving students some of the vocabulary associated with memorization is important. It takes the mystery out of the learning process and empowers the student.

In this section, I explore some general skills associated with memorization and then consider how to prepare for different kinds of tests.

28

Studying for Easy and Hard Subjects

Dear Teacher,

I find some subjects are much harder to study than others. English is really easy for me, but I have a lot of trouble with science. Why is that?

Sincerely,

It's So Hard

Dear It's,

Science is a very detailed subject. So are some other courses. You have to know every new vocabulary word and its definition, the structure and function, the cause and effect, or scientific concepts and specific examples of those concepts. Science, and courses like mathematics and foreign language, require what is sometimes called "verbatim memory." You have to memorize definitions and other concepts word for word (such as the exact English definition of a Spanish word). Although there are aspects of English that share these characteristics, literature is definitely different. Essentially, you need to remember the idea: the basic plot, what the character was doing, or what a particular metaphor represents. This subject needs a more general level of memory. You are not required to remember things word for word. Many students find one type of learning to be much easier than the other.

Good students learn to be adept at both kinds of memory. Verbatim memory requires the same approach to learning as information that is put into general memory; you just need to be more detailed. The letters in this section explore how to go about learning information in detail. If you can succeed in a course that requires verbatim memory, you can memorize information in *any* course you may take.

29

Overcoming Spelling Problems

Dear Teacher,

   I am a terrible speller. I am tired of losing points because I can't spell. What can I do?

Sincerely,

Kant Spel

Dear Kant,

I assume you do not have a learning disability that causes you to misspell words and that your problem with spelling is just a weakness you have not yet learned to overcome. Spelling words correctly is vital to being successful. Poor spelling can affect you in many unexpected ways. When I was hiring people and looked at job applications, if I saw a misspelled word, I quickly lost interest in the person and read no further. I thought that if the applicant was this careless about detail, my school would be the wrong place for that person. Spelling also plays an important role in communicating clearly to others. Misspelled words slow down the reader. Instead of following the point the writer was trying to make, now the reader has to stop and figure out what the word was supposed to be. At the very least, the reader's concentration is broken. I am glad you want to work on this problem.

There are several strategies that will help you. If you do your work on a computer and use a program that checks your spelling (such as "Spellcheck"), turn *off* the feature that automatically corrects misspelled words. Look at the way you spelled the word and how the program spells it. Monitoring yourself this way will help you learn how to spell words correctly.

When you are allowed to have someone help you with your work, ask your study skills coach to read over what you have written. When a misspelled word is found, he or she should circle it. Do not let your coach make the correction *for* you! The only way for you to learn to spell it correctly is to look up the word yourself.

The most important strategy is to study correct spelling when you do your homework or when you prepare for a test. Memorize how to spell a difficult word at the same time you memorize its definition. Practice saying and spelling the word out loud. Close your eyes and visualize the word as you say it. Try to "see" every letter. Write the word in big letters in the air. As you do, *subvocalize* each letter, saying them quietly to yourself, out loud. Do this several times. In the elementary grades, students are told to practice writing each spelling

Figure 29.1   A coach points out the errors but lets the student decide
how to correct them in this short essay.

My test is just a few days away. I <u>nead,</u> (spelling) to do well
on it or <u>eles</u> (spelling) my parents <u>willtake</u> (spelling) away
a privilege. I think they'll prevent <u>me</u> <u>and my friends</u> (<u>can</u>
<u>they do this to your friends?</u>) from going to the Mall after
school on Friday. So I need to start getting ready for the
test. I really need to get a high grade. (<u>redundant use of</u>
<u>the word *need*</u>)

word five times on a piece of paper. This is also an effective
technique. When you test yourself to see if you have begun to
store the vocabulary in your working memory, also check if
you have learned how to spell the word. Ask a friend to quiz
you on the spelling (working with your peers to improve your
spelling can be very helpful).

A coach can provide encouragement and support as you
strive to improve your spelling. Together, you should monitor
the number of spelling errors on your papers and tests. Your
goal is to reduce that number. Good luck! I am really pleased
that you want to overcome this problem. Good spelling will
serve you well all your life.

30

Is It Possible to Study Too Long for a Test?

Dear Teacher,

I studied for over three hours for my test. My friends only studied for about an hour. Do you think I'm overdoing it?

Sincerely,

Too Much

Dear Too,

Different people need different amounts of time to learn. Slow learners may need more than two nights of concentrated study in order to internalize the material being tested. I have had students who studied each night for five or more nights, getting ready for a test, because they wanted to improve their grade. That is a bit excessive, but they needed that extra time while they learned new study techniques (later on, they only prepped for two nights). For almost all students, I recommend that they start studying for a test early, spreading the process out over two nights. Extraordinarily fast learners are able to absorb information quickly and spend less than the average time preparing for a test. Also, we tend to find some subjects easier to study than others, and that affects how fast we learn. Researchers are beginning to discover some fascinating gender differences in the way we learn. Females, for example, learn words faster and retain them better than males (Gur, 2002; Ruben, 2002). This suggests that male students will have to spend longer studying vocabulary than female students. In general, however, most people need two days to prepare for a test, and that is what I recommend for you.

Regardless of the way you typically learn, I have some questions I need to ask. My first question is, are you wasting time? Perhaps you took over an hour rewriting your notes. This does not count as study time. (See my letter in Chapter 9, Note-Taking Formats, for help taking better notes, so you won't have to rewrite them.) Preparing study cards is not studying either; all you are doing is preparing the *tools* for studying. Another way students waste time is by allowing distractions. Some students open their book to begin studying and, within five minutes, receive the first of three phone calls, which take an hour to complete. These students return to their textbooks for 20 minutes, but then are called downstairs for dinner. Half an hour later, they go back to their rooms, but decide to check their e-mail . . . and on it goes. The student may *think* he or she spent three hours studying that night, but the truth is closer to half an hour.

I also want to ask, did you have all the materials you needed to study? Was your notebook well organized, or did you waste time looking for various papers? Did you study all of the right information or only some of it? Most important, how effectively did you study, that is, did you follow the strategies that I have been recommending? What I am trying to get at by asking these questions is that students often say they spend lengthy amounts of time studying for tests when, in truth, they use that time ineffectively. If you are throwing away precious time, I invite you to read the letters in this book with care so that you might learn how to manage your time and study with greater efficiency.

There is one more possible reason why you needed three hours to study for your test. If you do not need to spend an excessively long time to memorize information, if you had all your materials, if you truly used your time effectively, and, most important, you earned a high grade on that test, then I suspect you lack self-confidence and self-knowledge. Sometimes, very bright students are extremely anxious before a test. They work themselves up and put in more time preparing for it than is really needed. When they realize what they have done, they criticize themselves for "over-studying." If this describes you, then you need to know that you were not over-studying. What you did was to consolidate your knowledge, making your long-term memory stronger and stronger. There is nothing wrong with that, but once you really knew the material, you might have reduced the pressure you were putting on yourself. Instead of trying to keep on memorizing the material, all you needed to do was periodically test yourself to be sure you still retained it. With experience, you will learn how to cut back on the amount of time you devote to preparing for your tests. As you take more tests, you will better understand what to expect. I encourage you to identify how you might change how you study. Talk about this with your teacher or with a study coach; talking reduces anxiety and increases the control we have over our lives. If lack of confidence is causing you to spend too much time studying, then rest assured that you can overcome this problem.

31

Mnemonics

Dear Teacher,

What are mnemonics? How are they used?

Sincerely,

Strolling Down Memory Lane

Dear Strolling,

Mnemosyne was the Greek goddess of memory. Mnemonics are memory strategies that help students remember. There are several mnemonic strategies, all of which work because they give the information a handle by which it can be recalled.

One such strategy is called the *method of loci. Locus* means place, and this strategy involves visualizing something and then *placing* the things you are trying to learn in their proper locations. Imagine you had to study a map of the original thirteen colonies of the United States. Try to visualize the Eastern United States and on that mental image, locate each colony. This is an especially good technique for people who are artistic or who are visual thinkers.

Acrostics are sentences or phrases that utilize the first letters of the words you are trying to remember. "King Phillip Came Over for Good Spaghetti" is a classic acrostic often used by biology students to remember the classification system for organisms (**K**ingdom, **P**hylum, **C**lass, **O**rder, **G**enus, **S**pecies). Of course, acrostics work best when you make up the phrase or sentence yourself, because you will remember it most easily. If King Phillip does not mean much to you, you have the right to invent a new acrostic: "Kind People Came . . . etc." Try using acrostics when you have to memorize a series of related words. For example, if the words you are trying to learn are the names of the planets, an acrostic can be helpful. If you are trying to learn the names of totally unrelated items, however, acrostics will not work well.

Acronyms refer to words that are made up of selected letters from other words. NASA is the acronym for the National Aeronautics and Space Administration. The problem with acronyms is that if we want to share them with others, we can only use those that are known by everyone: FBI, GPS, or USA, for example. If you made up your own acronym, you would be unable to use it with anyone else; however, if you are only using acronyms to help you remember words, then coming up with your own acronyms can be quite powerful.

To make an acronym, write down the facts that you need to remember. Use the first letter of each word to make up the acronym. One well-known acronym is HOMES. It is used to remember the five Great Lakes: **H**uron, **O**ntario, **M**ichigan, **E**rie, and **S**uperior. Notice that the acronym is written in capital letters. If there is more than one word in a fact (such as White House), use only the first letter of the first word in the phrase (W). Sometimes two or more facts begin with the same first letter. In that case, you might use the first *two* letters of one of the facts (the second letter would be lowercased). For example, **CaCAD** is an acronym for seeds that are used in cooking: **Ca**raway, **C**elery, **A**nise, and **D**ill. As with acrostics, knowing an acronym is not enough. You also must know and remember what it represents. What good does it do if you only know that DNA stands for deoxyribonucleic acid? You must also know what those words mean and how DNA functions in protein formation.

Rhymes also make powerful mnemonics. Just think of the power of "i before e except after c," or "Thirty Days Hath September. . . ." Some students borrow songs, making up new words using the vocabulary they have to memorize. Just think what you could do with "Old MacDonald Had a Farm"!

Mnemonics, if not overused, are handy devices that put information into your memory and can then be used to recall it. Most people do not use them until they are having trouble absorbing related facts, when they just cannot seem to get the words into their heads. I suggest using mnemonics sparingly—but use them! They can really help.

32

Overwhelmed and Stuck

Dear Teacher,

Sometimes when I am doing my homework, especially my math homework, I'll look at a problem and become so overwhelmed that I don't know where to begin. Sometimes I'll try to find the answer four or five different ways, but I just can't seem to solve the problem. What's going on?

Sincerely,

Stuck

Dear Stuck,

In order to answer your question, I need to explain a bit about how your brain works. The brain is divided into two halves, or hemispheres (Wolfe, 2001b).

With remarkable consistency, the hemispheres show a preference or a bias toward certain activities (Wolfe, 2001a). For example, the left half of the brain tends to be more logical, sequential, and analytical. This hemisphere likes to find explanations as to why things occur, and it is the hemisphere we use when we draw very precise graphs of data. The right hemisphere is the side that looks at the total picture. We use this part of the brain to recognize faces or to look at and interpret a beautiful landscape.

Figure 32.1   The left and right hemispheres of the brain, with the cerebellum beneath them.

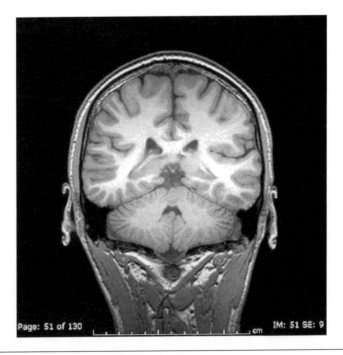

SOURCE: MRI Courtesy of Greenwich Hospital.

The two hemispheres are connected by a huge bundle of nerve cells so that they can communicate with each other. When we are faced with a problem, the hemisphere that prefers to work with that issue begins to solve it, but if the problem is too great, the other hemisphere becomes involved as well.

The situations you mentioned are very real and quite common. In the first situation, your right hemisphere began to work on the problem, but it could not detect the pattern that would tell it where to begin. When that happens, we say we are "right hemisphere stuck." In the second example, your left hemisphere tried to find the right sequence of steps that would produce a satisfactory solution, but nothing worked. When that happens, we say we are "left hemisphere stuck" (Jensen, 1997, 1998; Leonard, 2005). What you need in both cases is help from the other hemisphere, but in your examples, they did not communicate with each other.

To get unstuck, you need to know that the left hemisphere controls the right side of the body and the right hemisphere is responsible for the left side. To encourage the two sides of the brain to work together, place your right hand over your left shoulder, reaching as far as you can down your back. Return your right arm to your side. Now use your left hand to touch your back on the right side. Do this simple exercise five or six times, as quickly as you can. Alternatively, you could reach down behind you with your right hand as you raise your left foot behind you. Touch your hand to your heel. Do that five or six times with your right and left hands.

Not only does this little exercise help your hemispheres to communicate with each other, it also increases your circulation, which in turn brings more oxygen to your brain . . . and that is always good.

Return to the problem you are trying to solve. If this simple activity does not help, then make a note to ask your teacher for help.

33

Finding Clues About Test Content

Dear Teacher,

How can I get clues about what will be on the test?

Sincerely,

Clueless

Dear Clueless,

Let's start by looking for clues that are not included on the review sheet.

Students who are good listeners often pick up clues in class. Listen carefully to find out what teachers expect. They often tell you how to answer test questions. Do you have to use complete sentences? That tells you there will be free-response questions (essay or short answer). Listen to the teacher's voice. When emphasizing something important, teachers often slow down and speak more clearly. They may also change the volume of their voices. They often repeat the most important points to be sure students hear them. That should tell you these points are probably going to appear on the test. Listen to the questions teachers ask. They tend to ask about those things that are more important. Sometimes those questions are asked to prepare you for similar ones that will be on the test. You might be wise to write down the questions. Many teachers are in the habit of asking a question in class using the same words as the question on the test. As you listen to your teachers, mark your notes when you think something might appear on the test or quiz. I recommend you use a symbol such as the one I mentioned in Chapter 10, Note-Taking Shortcuts. Whether you use the symbol I suggest or your own, it will always mean *"This might be on the test!!"* Look at the questions at the end of the section or the end of the chapter in your textbook. Those are the questions the author thought were important. Those questions, or questions like them, might appear on your test.

Ask your teacher, "What will be the format of the test?" This information is important because you will study for a free-response (essay) test differently than you will for a test that consists of completion questions (fill-in-the-blanks).

Good students know how to predict what might be on the test. Weaker students need to practice this skill. I sense from your question that you need some practice. Students often find working in collaborative study groups before a test to be helpful (read my letter in Chapter 46, Study Groups). If you work with friends as part of your preparation for tests, try to predict the questions that you think will be on the test. You might hear someone say, "I think this will be on the test. Do you remember when she said . . .?"

If your teachers use review sheets, these are another excellent source of clues. When I was in grade school, I remember being given a list of words I had to memorize for spelling tests. Every word on the list would end up on the test the next day. However, as I got to the higher grades, the review sheets were more general. They just listed the concepts or topics I needed

Figure 33.1   You need to learn how to "work the review sheet," how to expand it from the teacher's simple listing of topics to study. You need to transform it into a more helpful tool. Notice the last two questions in each section. The student is trying to connect this course with the history course and with daily experiences. That is a powerful study technique.

Example of a Teacher's Review Sheet

Newton
Newton's First Law

Example of the Student's Expansion of That Review Sheet

Newton
- Birth date
- Lived in -?-
- Also known for -?-
- His contribution to our knowledge of motion?
- What else was happening in history at this time?

First Law
- This law states -?-
- Define inertia
- 2 examples of 1st law
- What causes a resting object to move?
- What causes a moving object to stop?
- What causes a moving object to change its motion?
- Why is this law important?
- When did I experience the 1st law on my bus ride home yesterday?

to know about. I had to know everything about those words, not just how to spell them. Certainly I had to be able to define the terms on the list, but I had to know much more than that. I had to understand the concepts. I had to be able to apply them to actual situations. I had to think of an example that would illustrate the concept or be able to recognize the concept in someone else's example. I had to find ways to connect one concept with another. I had to find the relationships between new concepts and those I had learned previously. In short, it was my responsibility to take the list my teacher had given me and learn everything I could about the terms that appeared on it. That review sheet was just a barebones outline; I was not given any hint as to *how* my teacher would test me on those questions (although I learned to listen carefully in class and gained insight that way). It was my job to know so much about the material that I could handle anything the teacher threw at me. In other words, it was my job to "work the review sheet."

So, start using that review sheet as the tool it was meant to be. Learn how to do this now, because later on, in more advanced courses, your teachers will not even hand out review sheets. They will assume you have learned to know what is important, and that you know how to make your own review sheets and will study them accordingly.

34

Study Cards

Dear Teacher,

I have never used review cards. I just make a few notes on the teacher's review sheet. But I have a friend who uses study cards, and she gets better grades. What are study cards, how do I make them, and how do I use them?

Sincerely,

Open to New Ideas

Dear Open,

I like your attitude. A willingness to try new things and a desire to improve is important.

Study cards are just tools, which, if properly designed and used, can improve a student's ability to study efficiently and effectively. Unfortunately, most students do not utilize the full potential of these tools.

Some students just write a list of words on a sheet of paper. I do not have anything against using paper instead of study cards, but a simple list of words leaves out all the other information that should also be memorized.

Another common error is to write down a word and immediately follow it with its definition. The problem with this is that the definition is written so close to the word that the student's eyes jump from the word to the definition. It is really hard to test ourselves on what we have learned when we are looking right at the answer.

An improvement on this approach involves drawing a line vertically down the center of the page. The student writes the word on the left side of the paper and its definition on the right side. The paper can be folded along the dividing line, thereby hiding the definition, and the student can review the words without accidentally glancing at the answers. The only problem with this technique is that the order of the list is fixed. The student cannot shuffle the list around in order to study.

I recommend that you use study cards (also called flash cards). Students who are just starting to learn how to use study cards often cram many words on one side and the answers on the reverse side. Use one card per term or concept. Novice students may write one word on one side and the answer on the reverse side, as shown in Figure 34.1. This is a good beginning, but we will take this study card and improve it.

This approach fails to make full use of study cards. A simple rephrasing is all it takes, however, to achieve the full power of the card. Instead of writing the word on one side, write it as a question. Instead of writing the answer as a statement, present it as a question, too.

Figure 34.1   A simple study card. While this is a good start, it is not the most useful type of study card.

Inertia	Tendency of an object that is at rest to remain at rest or that is in motion to remain in motion

Figure 34.2   This refined study card is really effective because it asks a question on both sides. Because this is just a study card and you are the only person who will see it, you do not have to be concerned that a question seems to be answered with another question.

What is inertia?	What is the tendency of an object at rest to remain at rest, or the tendency of an object that is in motion to remain in motion?

This simple little change allows you, when you test yourself, to answer the question on one side first, and then, a bit later, to use the other side to quiz yourself. This accomplishes several things. First, you are reinforcing what you have memorized when you test yourself with the question on the reverse side of the card. By presenting the same knowledge in slightly different formats, you are beginning to use "elaborative rehearsal techniques," the most powerful way to memorize (be sure to read my letter in Chapter 35, Long-Term Memory Formation).

You should not just write study cards for each word listed on a review sheet. You need to expand on that list (see my previous letter). For example, for the single word *inertia*, you might come up with more than half a dozen questions, as shown in Figure 34.3. Each question would be written on a separate card.

Figure 34.3   Seven questions that are developed from the single word
inertia. Each question would appear on a separate study
card, and the answers would be written as questions.

> What is inertia?
> What are two examples of inertia?
> A book is resting on the table. I push the book. Why is it
>   more difficult to start it moving than to keep it moving?
> I'm driving in a car. The brakes fail. Imagine the
>   road goes on forever, there is nothing in my
>   way, and there is no friction. What will happen?
> Use the word *acceleration* in the definition of inertia.
> Use the word *velocity* in the definition of inertia.
> How did I experience inertia on my way to school this morning?

These are just seven cards about inertia. You might think of a few more. Think of hypothetical questions. Ask yourself what if this concept *had* occurred. What if it were *not* true? What if this had *not* happened? Do not answer this kind of question with one simple sentence. Explain your thinking behind your answer. For example, if you asked what would happen if inertia did not exist, you would not just say that a sitting car would not be able to start moving. You must explain *why* it wouldn't move.

Use analogies. Ask yourself, "How is this like . . .?" For example, if you are studying history, you might ask, "How is the relationship between federal and state government like the structure of authority and responsibility in my school?" These are powerful techniques because they personalize the knowledge you are attaining, and that is what learning is all about.

You can write a review card for essay questions (and practice the answer) just as you would for a vocabulary word. When you write a card for this kind of question, however, you write only one question. Write the question on one side and write the key points you want to use to answer the question on the other side.

Each time you quiz yourself using your study cards, you should change the order of the cards. Flip the cards over and test yourself using the question on the reverse side (unless, of course, the card has an essay question).

Right about now, you are probably saying that this approach increases the amount of work you have to do. Actually, after you learn the answer to the primary question ("What is inertia?"), the others will come quite easily. Because you divided up your total learning about inertia into so many small pieces, each of which has greater and greater relevance, each piece is much easier to memorize than just a single definition might be. In the same way, once you learn the answers to the front sides of the cards, the answers to the questions on the reverse side can be memorized surprisingly quickly. What is most important is that, by the time you get done studying your cards, you will really understand the concept. If you measure how long you spend memorizing and weigh that time against how efficiently and more powerfully you are memorizing, you will find you use your time better and remember longer by using this elaborative memory technique.

One of the reasons why this technique works so well has to do with what happens when we memorize. Brain scientists have found that when we learn something, one brain cell reaches out and makes a connection with another cell. That connection, if it becomes permanent, is the physical equivalent of learning (Schenck & Kosik, 2000; Sprenger, 1999). Instead of activating a simple set of nerve cells that will just remember the definition, you caused your cells to branch out and network with many more cells. When you memorized the definition of inertia, a few cells linked up. When you used an example from your own experience, you linked that simple network containing the definition to cells that stored a memory of the experience. Memorizing is so much easier when you connect new words to things you already know. When you used the word *acceleration* in your definition of inertia, you linked your new word to a term you had already studied. You thereby succeeded in firmly attaching this new memory to many existing memories. For this reason, you will be much more likely to remember what inertia is when you take the test.

From a practical point of view, you have also prepared yourself to be able to answer a question correctly regardless of how the teacher asks it: fill-in-the-blank, multiple choice, matching columns, or whatever. Students are often confused when teachers present questions that require a concept to be applied to a totally new situation. You, however, will have the upper hand because you already practiced for those kinds of questions. In addition to memorizing the definition, you came up with a few examples of inertia. Even if the teacher uses a different example, you will be prepared and able to make the connection.

How does this work? Think of knowledge as involving increasing levels of complexity. Your first level of knowledge involves simple memory. Can you recite the definition of a word? A slightly more involved level is comprehension. Do you *understand* that definition? Can you explain it in your own words? Application is a still higher level of knowledge. You cannot comprehend something you have not learned, and you cannot apply it to new situations if you really do not understand the concept. Use of study cards in the manner I recommend prepares you for these higher-level questions.

In order to succeed with the kinds of questions your teacher gives you, you must first memorize the vocabulary. Then you have to explain it in your own words. Next, you have to illustrate the concept with examples and think how it is connected to other concepts you have learned. To test yourself and determine if you *really* know this new concept, there are several other strategies you can use. Read the next two letters to see how this is done.

I have one more recommendation. Do not throw your study cards away after the test. Save them. If you take exams or comprehensive tests, you will need them again.

35

Long-Term Memory Formation— Rehearsal and Recitation

Dear Teacher,

If I look for a few minutes at a word I need to memorize, I can remember it for a little while. But I usually can't remember it in an hour or so. Is this normal? How should I memorize for a test?

Sincerely,

Fond Memories

Dear Fond,

What you are experiencing is quite common. To understand it though, you need to know something about memory.

There are several kinds of memory. One is short-term memory (Huitt, 2003). It tends to last for only a few seconds or minutes. It is the kind of memory you use when you look up a telephone number; you hold onto the number in your head just long enough to make the call. You might be storing the words you are trying to learn in your short-term memory, but I think this is unlikely because you would have forgotten the word in just a matter of minutes. I think you are putting that word into working memory.

Working memory lasts for minutes to hours or days. This is the kind of memory that is used much of the time in school. Halfway through the class, you are still able to follow along because you remember how the class began and what has been said since. When you write, you are able to keep the main idea in your working memory as you develop a paragraph. When you cram for a test and try to learn that last vocabulary word before the teacher hands out the papers, you are using your working memory.

The problem with working memory is that it does not hold onto information very well. Working memory is like a temporary workspace. Things are held there only as long as the brain thinks it needs to work on the information. If a vocabulary word that you are trying to memorize is going to be lost from working memory, it will most likely be forgotten within the first 18 hours or so. This is so common that the experience has been given a name; it is called the *eighteen-hour rule* (Wolfe, 2001a). This is the reason why you might memorize material at night and think you really know everything, but when you wake up you discover you have forgotten some of it. I think this is what is happening to you. You are just storing information in your working memory, and then that memory begins to erode or fade . . . and yes, it is normal, although it is certainly not desirable.

Long-term memory is precisely what it sounds like. When information is stored there, you can recall the information months or years later. Your goal is to take material from your working memory, transfer it over to and register it in long-term memory, and then consolidate it. What I mean is that you want to place (register) the information in long-term memory and then, once it is there, you want to make it solid and strong (consolidate) so that it stays there, available for use on tests and later in the course.

Figure 35.1   Information held in working memory fades quickly. Placing the information into long-term memory, where it is stored for days, years, or even an entire lifetime, requires *registration* and *consolidation*.

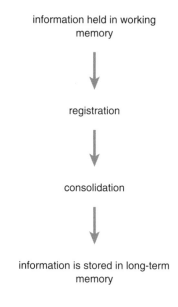

information held in working memory

registration

consolidation

information is stored in long-term memory

To place information into long-term memory, you need to rehearse and to use recitation. Let me explain. There are two kinds of rehearsal. The first is called *rote rehearsal.* This involves repeating the information or skill over and over again. It is how you might have learned to play a musical instrument. You practiced the skill repeatedly until you could do it without paying conscious attention. There isn't much thought involved. When I was in school, I used rote rehearsal to memorize the lines in a play. I would repeat them to myself many times until they sort of stuck in my mind. Rote rehearsal is fine for some things, but it is not a particularly effective way to study for most classes.

A more powerful technique is called *elaborative rehearsal.* This is the kind of studying I recommend. It is the type of memorization process I had in mind when I wrote to Open to New Ideas (about study cards) in the previous chapter. It allows you to elaborate on information in ways that give it meaning, enhance your understanding, and increase the likelihood you will retain it. It also makes the process of learning a bit more interesting.

Usually, we elaborate by giving the information *relevance,* or meaning, in our real lives. To do this, you need to connect the new information to previously learned knowledge and to other words and skills you are currently trying to internalize. For example, if you are learning the concept of inertia, you can connect it to your own experiences of riding in a car, and you can look for connections in other vocabulary words that will be on the test, such as *acceleration.* You can also draw a picture that shows the connections. Concept maps are graphic organizers that help you to see these relationships. Write the main idea in the middle of the page, and then branch each concept off from it. A concept map for the example I just gave is seen in Figure 35.2.

Concepts that are related along a particular branch could be coded in the same color. As you begin to see connections in a concept map, you will be able to write study cards that will really help you.

Elaborative rehearsal stores information in different parts of your brain. Science suggests that this is the best way to learn. We can take pictures of the brain using a technology called fMRI (functional magnetic resonance imaging). They show us the parts of the brain that become involved during certain activities. For example, when a person thinks about the word *toenail,*

Figure 35.2   A concept map that shows how different questions are connected to the concept of inertia.

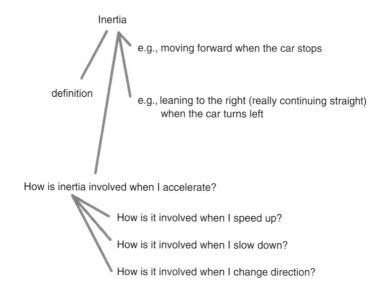

Inertia

definition

e.g., moving forward when the car stops

e.g., leaning to the right (really continuing straight) when the car turns left

How is inertia involved when I accelerate?

How is it involved when I speed up?

How is it involved when I slow down?

How is it involved when I change direction?

numerous areas in the brain light up on the fMRI image. This tells us we do not store the memory of a word in a single location in the brain (Fishback, 1999). Instead, we break it up and store it in numerous places. That is precisely what you want to do. When you look at a word and memorize it, you store the visual image in an area in the back of the brain that is associated with sight. When you write out the word, you store it in the area involved with muscular activity. When you say the word and its definition out loud, you will activate areas on the side of the brain that are involved in auditory storage. This is a rather simple explanation of a complicated process, but the point is that the more ways you memorize a concept, the more likely you are to remember it. If the memory disappears from one part of the brain, you have all those backup locations, and you will have greater success in recalling the information. What's more, by elaborating on the word in this way, you have a deeper and more solid understanding of the concept than if you had just memorized the definition. Because you used this elaborative technique, you can recall information more quickly and more accurately. Now that is a goal worth attaining!

Once you have learned the material, you should test yourself to determine if you really know it. By using your study cards, you quiz yourself in a process called *recitation.* I would highly recommend that you not rehearse the next set of concepts until you can answer these questions on the study cards. After memorizing the next words, you then recite all of the words you have learned so far, which reinforces your memory. In other words, you might rehearse and then recite the first five words. Then you rehearse the next four words. This time, you recite all nine words. And so on. Repetition and reinforcement are a powerful combination when it comes to memorizing.

The concepts we remember best tend to be the ones we studied first and last (Carraway, 2003; Sousa, 2001). For this reason, as you recite what you are trying to learn, shuffle your study cards so they are always in a different order. After you have recited the words on one side of the study card, turn it over so you will have to answer the opposing question. This really strengthens your memory.

I *strongly* recommend that you recite out loud. In fact, I cannot emphasize this strongly enough. You need to be able to *hear* if you know the material. If you do not vocalize what you are memorizing and only think through the recitation process, your brain, which does not want to learn and does not like working so slowly, might jump over a few details. (You might read back over my letter in Chapter 14, Why Even Do Homework?) You will think you know all the information, but because you did not focus on the details by saying them out loud, you might discover you did not know them as well as you thought you did.

If you think about it, this is how actors learn the lines of a play. They memorize a few lines and recite them out loud. Then they learn a few more lines and recite all of them. Why should learning for a test be any different? I recommend you pretend you are talking to someone, perhaps even teaching an imaginary student, while you recite. Pretend you are the teacher. Pretend you are a television host explaining what you are learning to an imaginary audience. You have to talk clearly and give a precise and intelligent explanation. You can even work with your coach and explain the concepts you have memorized. Teaching someone else is a very powerful way to find out if you really know the material and understand it.

To understand why elaboration and reciting out loud works, you need to know how your brain responds to information. If you simply listen to a teacher talk, you might remember about 7% of what was said. If you listen and take notes about the material, you will remember roughly 10%. If you see a picture, you will recall 20%, and if the information is demonstrated, you are likely to recall about 30%. If you come up with your own example of a concept, there is a 12% increase in the likelihood you will remember it. If you practice by doing, your ability to retain information jumps to 75%, and if you teach someone else, you will remember about 90% of the information (Carraway, 2003; Sousa, 2001). This is why reciting out loud is such a powerful technique. You want to end up in that 90% bracket!

When you test yourself, or recite, you might try standing up and moving around. The part of the brain that is involved in coordinating your muscles and helping you to keep your balance is the cerebellum. It is located in the bottom rear area of your brain. Until fairly recently, muscle coordination and balance were the only things scientists thought this part of the brain controlled. But new technology allowed them to discover, much to their surprise, that it has many other functions as well (Bower & Parsons, 2003; Jensen, 2000; Leiner & Leiner, 2002). The cerebellum is involved in word selection, judging the shape of objects, sequencing, attention, creating properly proportioned drawings, and even decision making. Scientists are now convinced there are links that connect movement and thinking. There is quite a lot of research that suggests that physical activity improves the effectiveness with which a person learns. Scientists have discovered that moving while talking helps people to hold onto information longer. I cannot stress enough the importance of movement while you memorize and recite. I just wish all the strategies and tricks to strengthen our memory were this easy!

There are other strategies that you can use that combine movement and memorization. As you memorize a vocabulary word, close your eyes, visualize the word, and draw the word in the air. Mentally visualize the word as you write it with your eyes closed. If you are trying to memorize a sequence of events, such as the life cycle of a butterfly, move your hands in the air from one part of the sequence to the next as if you were drawing the cycle on the board.

Information is moved into long-term memory when it is repeated many times during the learning process. It is more likely to remain there if that information is given relevance. As you continue to recite the term, the memory is strengthened, or *consolidated*. It is further consolidated if you start the memorization process a couple of days before the test. When you return to the material the next night, the memory will be made even stronger.

36

Memorizing Long Lists

Dear Teacher,

I find memorizing long lists of words to be really hard. Why is that?

Sincerely,

Unlisted

Dear Unlisted,

The reason long lists are hard to memorize is because you do not have enough *functional capacity*, that is, your brain can only handle a certain amount of information at a time when you are trying to memorize (Cowan, 2001; Wolfe, 2001a). That amount is fairly small. When you were 5 years old, you could memorize about two to four items at a time. That number increased to three to five items by age 7, and it will reach its maximum by age 15. At that point, you will be able to handle seven items, plus or minus two.

Because of this limited functional capacity, it is best to divide long lists into small pieces. Instead of trying to tackle a long list all at once, you may start just by memorizing and rehearsing four easy pieces of information. Four terms do not exceed your functional capacity. Once you think you know them, recite them out loud. The recitation process is like pushing a reset button. It allows your brain to start anew. After you have stored the information in your working memory, you might learn the next few words. This time, you may decide to memorize only two words because they are difficult concepts. As you know if you read my letter to Fond Memories in the previous chapter, it is best to recite the six items and learn them before memorizing the next few words. In this way, you work your way down the list, never over-taxing your functional capacity.

Breaking a list up into smaller pieces is called *chunking*. But there is more to chunking than just dividing a list up into manageable lengths. You need to organize the information in ways that are meaningful or relevant. You need to group the information into recognizable patterns. Your brain loves to find patterns (Jensen, 1998). When you were little, did you ever look at drawings with "hidden pictures" and try to find the objects hidden in them. Perhaps a tree had an umbrella hidden in the lines of the trunk or a rock disguised a fox. Do you like walking on the beach and looking for sea glass while ignoring all the other items that have washed up? You enjoy doing these things because your brain likes patterns. When you chunk a list and make meaningful patterns, your brain will find memorizing to be easier. One pattern you might create is grouping the words on the list according to how they are connected. In my letter in Chapter 31, Mnemonics, I showed how to use a concept map to illustrate those connections.

In addition to being limited by your functional capacity, your ability to handle information is also limited by time. You can concentrate and effectively pay the total attention required for memorization only for short periods. Your brain does a poor job at tasks that demand focused attention for long periods. It pays attention for a limited time, after which it needs a break. Preadolescents can pay close attention for roughly 5 to 10 minutes, and adults can focus intensely for 10 to 20 minutes before becoming fatigued. After that, the brain needs a short rest. Furthermore, as you become tired, the length of time you can concentrate decreases (which is why, in my letter in Chapter 20, Homework Schedules, I suggested increasing the length of breaks as the evening wore on). This is one of the reasons cramming—studying at the last minute and trying to stuff too much information into your working memory—does not work effectively.

I recommend you study in chunked amounts of limited size. Memorize about five items at a time by saying them over and over to yourself. This is called rehearsal. Once you think you have memorized them, test yourself. Recite the answers out loud. Then memorize the next chunked set of five words. This time, recite all 10 words, then all 15, all 20, and so on. Notice that you are reinforcing what you have learned each time you recite the information. By breaking up the memorizing/ rehearsal process with recitation/repetition, you have given your brain the break it needs from intense focusing.

I also recommend that you think about what time of night you should memorize material for a test. As the evening goes on, you get more tired and your brain learns more slowly. Just as I've suggested that you study the hardest, most demanding subjects earlier in the evening, it is also a good idea to work on your memorization tasks at this time, when your brain is freshest. Studying for a test should also be done as early as possible. Then tackle the easier subjects later in the evening. After you have finished your homework, you can return to your study cards and test yourself one last time.

37

Forgetting and Cramming

Dear Teacher,

I knew the material last night. My father even quizzed me on it and he said I knew it. But I did poorly on the test. What's going on?

Sincerely,

Dad's Upset

Dear Dad's,

What a good question! But before I answer it, I want you to focus on your name. Although your question suggests that you want to know what is happening, the name you chose for yourself makes me wonder whether your father is more concerned than you. Until *you* are upset, until you are willing to own your problem and do what it takes to find a solution, things will not change very much. But I'm going to assume you do want to improve your study strategies.

Part of the problem that you experienced may have to do with the way you were quizzed. I wonder if you memorized only the terms on the review sheet. I wonder if your father then took the review sheet and asked about examples he had made up, rephrased information in his own way, and connected different words on the sheet when he saw patterns and relationships. If this is how he tested you, then he was the person who was engaged in the review sheet, not you. You were just reacting to your father. You were not making all of the connections in your brain that are a vital part of learning (read my previous two letters). You had missed an opportunity.

Now let's assume you studied all the right material in the way I recommend, using elaborative rehearsal and recitation techniques. What you are asking is how could you know the material at night, when your father quizzed you, and then forget some of it by the time you took your test. The answer lies in how your brain works and how brain scientists think we learn (or memorize).

As I've mentioned in other letters in this book, working memory does not last very long—just minutes to hours, or perhaps as long as several days. Long-term memory lasts for months and maybe even for our lifetime. You use working memory when you speak. You hold the beginning of the sentence in working memory as you come up with the necessary words to complete the thought. You also use your working memory when you watch a movie. As you reach the end of the story, you are able remember what you had seen at the beginning. When you begin to memorize something, your brain first puts that material into working memory. Unfortunately, you did not transfer the material you were trying to learn over to long-term memory.

When you put a lot of information into working memory in a limited time and do not give it a chance to be consolidated into long-term memory, you are doing what's called *cramming*.

The problem is that working memory fades fairly quickly (Schenck & Kosik, 2000). As you know if you read my letter in Chapter 35, Long-Term Memory Formation, you begin to forget material within 18 to 24 hours unless you keep working at it and reinforce that memory. To avoid this problem, you need to study the material some more so that your brain begins the process of consolidation, transferring the information from working memory to long-term memory.

I suspect what you had done was just to put the material into your working memory. You successfully got through the evening and your father's testing. Then you went to sleep, and your brain started to forget bits and pieces of what you had learned. By the time you woke in the morning and went down to breakfast, you might have had the uneasy feeling that you no longer knew everything quite so well. Then you went to school, caught up with your friends, and went to a few classes. By the time you took your test, a significant amount of information had been lost from your working memory.

The good news is, you can help your working memory hold onto the information for longer amounts of time and help your brain send it to long-term storage. Don't wait until the night before the test to begin to memorize the material. Start two or more nights before the test. If you read my letters about the memorization process (Chapter 35), you know that the more times you recite, repeat, and reinforce information that you have made relevant, the better you will remember it. You need to start your memorization process earlier in order to give your brain the time it needs to consolidate that information. Your goal should be to retain the information at least for several days, not just several hours.

I often tell students that learning is the hardest thing we do in schools. I am not just being flippant when I say that. The cold, hard truth is that learning and memorizing take a lot of effort. Give yourself enough time to learn the material, to make the necessary effort, and it will pay off. You'll learn things better and remember them longer.

38

Directives

Dear Teacher,

My teacher returned my test and said I did not know what "compare and contrast" meant. Okay, so what does it mean?

Sincerely,

COMPARison Shopper

Dear COMPARison,

Terms like *compare and contrast* are called directives. They tell you how to answer test questions. Let me help you understand some of the more common directives.

Compare tells you to look at the similarities shared by two or more items. Ask yourself what they have in common. *Contrast* directs you to write about the differences between two or more items. *Compare and contrast,* therefore, asks to you explore both the similarities and differences between two or more concepts. Look for cue words as you read a text or listen to your teacher. When concepts are similar, you will probably see words such as *also, just as, like, likewise,* or *in the same way.* When concepts are different, you will see *however, although, whereas,* or *on the other hand.* When you take notes or annotate your text, write the words *compare* or *contrast,* as appropriate, in the Review column of your Cornell method notes or the margin of the book (if you are allowed to write in your book).

One way to take compare and contrast notes is to use a Venn diagram. A Venn diagram is just another type of graphic organizer in which you can record the similarities and differences.

Figure 38.1   A Venn diagram allows a student to organize ideas visually. Similarities are recorded in the area in which the circles overlap. The differences lie outside this common area.

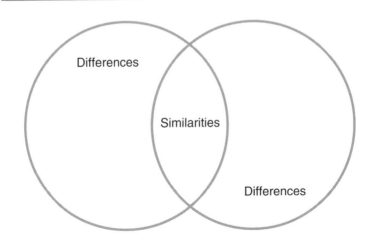

Figure 38.2   Cause and effect boxes help you to see the relationship.

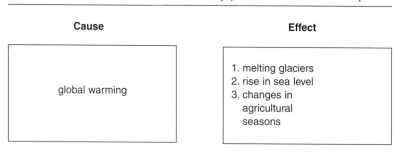

Once you have organized the information you need in a Venn diagram, you can study for your test and prepare for probable essay questions.

You can prepare for *cause and effect* questions in much the same way. A *cause* makes something happen. The *effect* is the consequence of that cause. There are certain words that are used to indicate you are looking at a *cause and effect* relationship: *because, so, since, therefore, results in, leads to,* and, of course, *cause.* You can use two boxes to graphically organize your thoughts as you study for this kind of question.

Define is a directive that tells you the teacher is looking for a clear, concise meaning of a term. Examples may not be required, but they often help convey the message that you know what you are talking about (so do labeled drawings).

Discuss asks you to analyze an issue carefully. In your answer, be sure to define any new terms you might use.

Evaluate is a directive that asks you to explore both sides of an issue, to present the positive and negative sides, and then to evaluate them and say which one is better, and why.

List tells you to do just that: to present a numbered list. If you are asked to list events in sequence or in chronological order, you must list them in the order in which they happen.

Summarize is a directive that asks you to present the main points in a very succinct manner.

There are other directives, but these are more than enough to get you started. Use these terms when you prepare for possible free-response questions (short answer or essay questions).

Figure 38.3   Directives guide you and tell you how the teacher
                    wants you to answer a question.

Directives	
Compare	- identify the similarities
Contrast	- identify the differences
Compare and Contrast	- identify both the similarities and differences
Cause	- identify the factors responsible for making an event happen
Effect	- identify the consequences of an event
Define	- give the meaning of a term
Discuss	- analyze an issue, defining new terms as they are used
Evaluate	- explore both sides of an issue and state why one is better
List	- provide a numbered list
Summarize	- state the main points in a highly condensed answer

When studying for a test, write down some ideas that give
you a good answer and then review them as you would any
other possible type of essay question.

39

Food for the Brain

Dear Teacher,

I have been told that fish is brain food. Is there really a connection between what I eat and how I do on my tests?

Sincerely,

Upscale

Dear Upscale,

Research has found that what you eat does affect your brain. Dehydration is a common problem linked to poor learning. Scientists can see a positive change in the brain within five minutes of drinking water because the level of a brain chemical called cortisol is reduced (Carraway, 2003; Gurian & Stevens, 2005). Cortisol is produced when you experience stress (dehydration stresses your body), and it interferes with your ability to learn. Water is also important to the brain because its cells work in a liquid environment. You may have heard that you should drink an average of 8 to 10 glasses of water a day for optimum brain activity. Of course, you get some water from the food you eat. Coffee and other caffeine-containing beverages do not count because caffeine is a *diuretic*, which means it pulls water out of the body. Sugar-based sodas contain so much sugar that they, too, cause you to lose water from your body. So stop at the water fountain on your way to take a test! And make sure you get your 8 to 10 glasses a day.

Like water, the food you eat has been found to affect the brain (Ratey, 2001; Sousa, 2001; Sprenger, 1999). Scientists have found that meals rich in carbohydrates and low in proteins increase the amount of a chemical called serotonin in the brain. This chemical causes a relaxed or sleepy state of mind in which your reaction time is slowed. Students who eat carbohydrate-rich lunches before an afternoon test might lose their edge. A meal that is rich in protein causes the brain to release a chemical called norepinephrine. It helps you to be more alert and to make decisions under pressure. That is the kind of meal you want to have before a test! Of course, if you haven't studied and you do not know the material, it does not matter what you eat or drink. You will still do poorly.

I am deeply concerned about students who do not eat breakfast. Their brains have gone without nourishment for at least eight hours while they slept. Now they have to cope with the demands of school, but their brains lack the energy to function at optimal levels. Many years ago, scientists found that students who avoid breakfast earn grade averages that are

Figure 39.1   Food and nutrients that help you to learn.

Foods Rich in Protein

Beans
Cereal with milk
Chicken
Eggs
Fish
Nuts
Seeds
Steak
Whole grains

about 10 points lower than the population of students who eat well-balanced meals three times a day (Howard, 2006; Pollitt & Matthews, 1998; Powell, Walker, Chang, & Grantham-McGregor, 1998). Eating breakfast is a practically effortless way to improve one's grades.

Sometimes I hear students complain that they do not want breakfast because they are on a diet. These students misunderstand how diets work. They need to consider their caloric intake over 24 hours, not just at any particular meal. This means they can have a small breakfast and then reduce the number of calories they consume for the rest of the day by a comparable amount. They can remain on their diet and still have the breakfast they need to start their day.

I also hear students say they do not have time for breakfast in the morning. That's absurd! How long does it take to drink a glass of milk, eat a piece of toast, and grab an apple to eat on the way? Breakfast does not have to be a huge meal. Using lack of time as an excuse is an example of *rationalization* ("Defense Mechanisms," n.d.). On the surface, this excuse *seems* sensible, but it really is not. Rationalization is a behavior that allows people to avoid dealing with the truth. The fact is that students who do not eat something for breakfast are simply not taking care of themselves because they are not getting a good nutritional start each day. I am concerned that they are preventing themselves from reaching their full academic potential. I hope you are someone who makes a point of eating breakfast every day.

Yes, Upscale, your brain really is affected by what you eat. It works best when you eat properly. When your brain has what it needs to operate well, you have a better chance of learning more easily and earning stronger grades.

40

Preparing for Free-Response Questions

Dear Teacher,

Do you have any tips that will help me do better on essay and short-answer questions?

Sincerely,

Trouble With Prose

Dear Trouble,

Essays and short answers are called *free-response questions,* a term that implies that you, the writer, are in charge of how to present the answer.

My first suggestion is to develop the habit of trying to predict the questions the teacher might ask and to outline possible answers as you study. Not only will this strategy help you prepare for free-response questions, it will also help you to consolidate the information in your brain.

Before you begin to write an essay or short answer test, read the directions carefully. Do you have to answer every question, or do you have to answer only a certain number from the choices that have been provided? Later, when you have finished writing, quickly count to double-check that you answered the correct number of questions. Students who fail to do this sometimes skip a question and lose points. Even worse, some students answer too many questions and then run out of time.

Pay attention to how the question is phrased, and look at the directives (review my letter in Chapter 38, Directives). Quickly jot down key words and ideas that you want to weave into your essay so you won't forget them as you write.

If you are given 40 minutes in which to write three essays, allow yourself only 10 minutes for each answer. This gives you time to gather your thoughts before you start writing and time to proofread after you are done. If you have given yourself 10 minutes in which to write an essay, stop when the time is up. Leave plenty of space on your paper so you can return to that answer if time permits, but go on to the next question. In this way, you will have answered each question, at least in part, when the time is up. Incomplete answers usually receive more credit than a totally unanswered one. If you return to an essay and still do not have enough time to write a full answer, use an outline to record your remaining thoughts. An outline is not the same as an essay, but you may receive some credit for indicating that you knew the answer, and even if your teacher does not give you any credit, you will have every right to feel better because you showed yourself that you had studied successfully.

Write neatly. You might lose points if your teacher cannot read what you wrote. Unless told to do so, do not waste precious writing time by rewriting the question. Get right to the point, and be concise. If you use a diagram to help explain what you are writing, either give it a caption or refer to it in your answer. A picture without any supporting text is usually meaningless and won't get much or any credit. Finally, when you are finished, proofread carefully for errors (read my letter in Chapter 45, Proofreading).

41

Preparing for True/False Tests

Dear Teacher,

I don't do that well at true/false questions. How can I get better at answering them? How should I approach true/false questions?

Sincerely,

Searching for the Truth

Dear Searching,

My first recommendation is to read the directions carefully. If the statement is true, are you supposed to leave the answer space blank, write *true*, or enter the letter *T*? When the statement is false, some teachers tell you to correct the statement to make it true instead of writing *false* or the letter *F*. Following directions correctly is part of the test-taking procedure.

There are some tricks you should know that can improve your chances of doing well on true/false questions. If any part of the answer is false, even if everything else is true, then your response must be *false*.

The use of negatives (such as *cannot, does not, is not, no, not*) can make the question confusing. Read the sentence without the negatives and decide whether the statement, as read, is true or not. If you decide it is true, its negative is usually false.

Qualifiers like *sometimes, often, frequently, rarely,* or *usually* are used because the teacher knows there may be an exception and is being careful to make a correct statement. When you see one of these words, slow down and think carefully about the accuracy of the sentence.

Absolutes like *always* (or *never*) imply the statement must be true forever. Forever is a very long time, and the answer is often false.

If you truly have no idea whatsoever, as a last resort you can guess the answer. After all, you have a 50% chance of guessing it right.

42

Preparing for Multiple-Choice Questions

Dear Teacher,

Do you have any hints that might help me with multiple-choice questions?

Sincerely,

M.C.

Dear M.C.,

Most multiple-choice questions consist of a *stem* followed by choices that include the correct answer and three or four incorrect answers, also called *distractors*. There are some things you should find out from the teacher before you begin to answer the questions. Does each question have only one correct answer? Will you be penalized if you choose the wrong answer? Some tests deduct one point for the wrong answer and only a quarter-point if you leave the answer blank. In that case, you would be better off not answering a question at all than answering it incorrectly. Fewer points would be deducted for a blank space than for an incorrect response.

If you do not know the answer, eliminate any choices that you know are incorrect. That increases the probability of selecting the correct choice. Then use these tricks: Any possible answer that does not grammatically agree with the stem is probably incorrect. Choices that include absolutes like *always* or *never* are often incorrect. Similarly, choices containing qualifiers like *sometimes*, *seldom*, or *usually* are more likely to be correct. Choices that are long and give the most thorough explanation are often right—though not always.

Of course, none of these tricks will help you if you have not studied properly; they are just designed to give you an additional edge.

Figure 42.1   The question is called the *stem*. Answer B is correct.
Answers A, C, and D are *distractors*.

What is the tendency of
an object to remain at rest?
A. gravitation
B. inertia
C. force
D. momentum

43

Preparing for Open-Book Tests

Dear Teacher,

I've heard that an open-book test can be very hard. Is this true?

Sincerely,

Open and Shut

Dear Open,

One of the greatest mistakes students make regarding open-book tests is to not study for them. They think that they do not have to prepare for the test since they will be allowed to refer to their text or notes. The problem with this strategy is that time is usually very limited on these tests. Students who have to constantly look things up waste time that would have been better spent answering questions.

You should study for open-book tests much as you would for any other test. Commit the material to memory. Most open-book tests will have free-response questions (but ask your teacher about the test format, anyway), so try to anticipate the topics you will have to write about and study accordingly. When you prepare for an open-book test, organize your text and notes beforehand. Anticipate the questions the teacher is most likely to ask and know where the information or quotes that you will need are located so you can turn to them in a hurry. You might even mark their location using sticky notes.

44

Problems Finishing the Test

Dear Teacher,

Sometimes I don't finish a test. I know it is my problem because everyone else finished on time. What can I do?

Sincerely,

Seemingly Slow

Dear Seemingly,

I really like the way you are taking ownership of your problem! Some students process slowly. They read questions slowly, think slowly, and answer the questions slowly. These students might need extended time on their tests and specialized help in order to speed up the way their brains process information. If you think this describes you, you need to talk with your teacher.

But let's assume you do not fall into this category. Some students feel compelled to answer the questions in the order in which they appear on the test, and they may become stuck on a particularly challenging one. They spend so much time on that one question that they run out of time and are then unable to answer the last five. In other words, they spend too long on a five-point question, and then lose 25 points because they did not answer those last five questions. If this describes you, I suggest that you skip that difficult question as soon as you realize you are having trouble with it. Finish the test and come back to it later.

I also suggest that you skip around on the test. Don't worry if your friends work straight through their tests. You need to take a different approach. Answer the easiest questions first. Then tackle the ones you find difficult. If one of those questions is an essay question and you find yourself running out of time, stop writing sentences and start conveying your knowledge in an outline form. Also, you should not spend too much time making sure you phrased everything perfectly, used exactly the right word to express your thoughts, and had absolutely perfect grammar. This is a test of what you know, not an essay that you write at home, where you have the luxury of rewriting. Although good writing is a commendable goal, your desire to finish the test is more important, at least at the moment. Go back and check only those questions that were difficult for you. Do not waste time proofreading answers that you know are correct (read the letter in the next chapter).

Being aware that you have trouble finishing tests is an important step, and your desire to improve is also important.

You are clearly motivated to improve and to change. Being aware of what causes you to slow down while you take a test and knowing the strategies to overcome the problem is the first step on the road to improvement and success. Good luck!

45

Proofreading

Dear Teacher,

My teacher keeps telling me I should proofread my answers on my tests, but I do look over my answers. How can I do a better job at proofreading?

Sincerely,

Catching Errors

Dear Catching,

Proofreading is hard, regardless whether you are proofing a test or a paper that you have written. Part of the problem you face when you proofread your papers or test answers is that you need to look for several kinds of errors: factual, spelling, grammatical, and syntax errors. Catching spelling errors can be particularly difficult. If you did not know how to spell a word correctly in the first place, you will probably not recognize that it is misspelled when you proofread. Determining whether you accurately conveyed your thinking is the greatest challenge you face when you proofread. Unfortunately, you know what you meant as you wrote it, and that skews your ability to proofread objectively. The longer you can put a paper off to the side before you proofread it, the more productive the experience will be because you will have a chance to step back and regain your objectivity. I know this is hard to do. In school, teachers tend to assign one paper right after the other, and it is difficult to get that distance. It is even harder on tests because of the time constraints. Nevertheless, you have to do the best you can, and there are some proofreading skills you can use as you focus on this task.

First, recognize what you are looking for as you proofread. If you are looking for factual errors, read the passage through from beginning to end. Make sure you presented all of the required information in the proper order. Did you use appropriate examples? Could you have benefited from using a diagram, and if you used one, did you add an appropriate caption? Did you provide the necessary references or quotes?

Second, read for spelling errors. One neat little trick is to read your paper backwards, from the last to the first word. Editors sometimes do this because they know how easy it is to let our eyes slide over words as we read, thereby missing errors. By reading backwards, you are more likely to notice each and every word.

When you read for syntax and meaning you are checking that you used proper grammar, the best word to convey your thought, and that you wrote clearly and concisely so the reader will understand what you are thinking. Reading aloud or subvocalizing is a good trick to use, especially if you keep your intended audience in mind. It helps you to detect confused or incomplete thinking.

Finally, if you are writing a paper at home and your teacher permits it, ask a parent or friend to act as a coach and to look over your paper, but only after you have proofread the material yourself. Do not let the other person make any corrections; that is your job. The friend or parent should just circle any error or put a question mark beside any passage that is confusing.

Proofreading is hard, but it is a kind service you do for your readers. Whether you are writing an essay on a test or a paper at home, by proofreading, you try to make it easier for your intended audience to understand what you have written. Proofreading is actually the final step of the writing process (Zinsser,1990). It tells you what needs to be changed in order to have the writing make more sense and be more readable.

46

Study Groups

Dear Teacher,

I like to study for tests with my friends. One of my teachers says this is a bad idea, while another teacher says it's just fine. Who is right?

Sincerely,

Caught Between Two Teachers

Dear Caught,

One reason that study groups often do not succeed is because the members of the group can forget why they came together. Instead of studying, they begin to talk about social matters—they gossip, tell stories, and laugh. At this point, the group has lost its focus. If this is what is happening in your group, then your first teacher is correct.

Study groups can be very helpful, however. If used well, they can actually strengthen your learning. What makes a successful study group? Study groups are a special kind of cooperative group in which each member of the team supports and relies upon every other member. Everyone is there to learn, and everyone is an active participant. Each student contributes. If someone comes to the group just to listen and absorb information, that person is not helping everyone else and should be asked to start sharing or leave the group.

Study groups should consist of no more than three to five students. In a small group, everyone can have a meaningful role, and small groups are easier to keep on track.

Study groups should set clear goals and expectations. Everyone should study the material before coming to the group. If someone does not come prepared to do the work, that person should be excused from the group. Study groups are not substitutes for students' own study, however. They should be used to enhance, or add to, the studying each student is doing on his or her own.

Here are some suggested guidelines for an effective study group: A group member can ask questions about any subject or concept he or she is having difficulty understanding, and the group will help that person. Each member can ask the group questions from his or her own study cards and help the group learn the answers. One particularly effective activity for study groups involves predicting possible free-response questions and thinking about the key points that will be needed to answer them.

The group meetings should be scheduled so that each member will have time to do some more studying on his or her own before the test or exam. Study groups are most effective when they are used to prepare for major tests or exams, not quizzes or tests on short units. These short assessments do not cover as much, and students should be able to prepare for them on their own.

I hope these guidelines help you, Caught. If you do work in a study group, and if everyone in it stays focused and on task, pat yourself on the back because you are seeing another sign that you are growing up, gaining maturity, and becoming more responsible.

47

Remembering Locations— Episodic Memory

Dear Teacher,

When I take a test, I sometimes try to remember where I saw the answer in the textbook. Is this a good technique?

Sincerely,

Where It's At

Dear Where,

You are talking about something called *episodic memory.* This kind of memory is prompted by location or circumstance (Sprenger, 1999). Most of us remember exactly where we were when we heard about the 9/11 attacks. This is an example of episodic memory.

You are tapping into episodic memory when you try to visualize the page in the book that had the information you are trying to recall. You could also look at the space on the bulletin board where the teacher had hung a poster or try to remember where the teacher was standing when a certain concept was being taught. Episodic memory is so strong that we often do better if we take the test while sitting in the same seat we occupied while the unit was being taught.

If you plan to use episodic memory during a test to help you remember things, you should also study that way. As you use elaborative rehearsal techniques (see Chapter 35), memorize the locations: Where was the picture in the text? What was the message next to the map that hung on the wall? Where did the information appear in your notebook? This will help your recall.

You should also use pictures when you study. We remember pictures better than diagrams, diagrams better than symbols, and symbols better than words (Carraway, 2003; Wolfe, 2005). If you cannot draw a picture and then explain it, create a mental picture and talk about it.

48

Should You Keep Your Eyes on Your Paper?

Dear Teacher,

My teacher tells me not to look around the room while I take a test. I find it very hard not to look up from time to time. What should I do?

Sincerely,

Just Looking

Dear Just,

Assuming you never look anywhere near a neighbor's test paper, I think you should be proactive. Advocate for yourself; talk with your teacher and explain what you do. If necessary, offer to close your eyes when you look away from your test.

You raise an interesting question: will looking around help you on your test? Read my previous letter about episodic memory. There is another type of *looking* you should know about. For most people, about 90% of the population, looking in a specific direction actually helps them think and remember things (Siegel, 2003). Sometimes your brain needs help to recall information it has stored in memory. Brain research has shown that if you look up and to the left, you might be able to access visual information just a bit more easily (Conyers & Wilson, 2001). This might be helpful when you are trying to remember how to label a diagram or a map.

Do you want to see this in action? Ask a friend, "How many windows are there on the north side of your house?" Watch where your friend's eyes look immediately after you asked the question! Looking up and to the right helps to put you in touch with your visual imagination. This can help when you are writing a piece of fiction and you need to be imaginative. Looking across and to the left helps with auditory recall ("What did the teacher say again?"), and across and to the right touches on auditory imagination. Looking down and to the left helps you monitor what you are saying ("Does this make sense?"), while looking down and to the right puts you in touch with memories of physical motion ("How did I set up that lab equipment?").

The savvy test-taker knows better than to "keep his eye on his paper." But make sure you talk to your teacher first so he or she knows your eyes are "wandering" in the right direction and with a good purpose!

49

Analyzing Returned Tests

Dear Teacher,

   Is there anything special I should do when the teacher returns my test?

Sincerely,

Am I Done Yet?

Dear Am I,

What a great question! Too many students just look at their grade and then put the test in their notebook (or worse, the trash can). But the learning process did not end when you took the test. You have a bit more work to do.

In addition to correcting your errors—which reinforces your memory—analyze your test to determine why you made your mistakes. As I mentioned earlier in the book, the brain loves to find patterns, and this is what you need to do to make sure you don't make the same kinds of mistakes again. Did your errors fall into a particular pattern?

As you look over your test, ask yourself, were the errors caused by a failure to read and follow directions carefully? If so, learn to circle key words in the directions as you read them. After you have read the first question on a test, go back and re-read the directions to be sure you really understood them.

Did you find you had trouble with questions that asked about dates? Try spending more time memorizing them as you study for your next test.

Do not just look for your weaknesses; also find your areas of strength. Look for evidence that the study strategies you are trying to learn are paying off. I can't emphasize enough how important positive reinforcement and praise are in life!

PART V

Exams

Exams are unique. Yes, they are just large tests, but they can do things that unit tests cannot accomplish. Exams go much further than covering more material and probing the student's ability to handle large volumes of information. Exams tie units together. They can look at those units thematically, and they can apply concepts learned in one unit to those learned in other areas of the course. They enable the learner to look at material from new vantage points. They encourage even greater consolidation of information into long-term memory as the student reviews. All of the skills that have been learned for quizzes and tests suddenly become extraordinarily important. Hopefully, these skills have been internalized and will become solid habits before students have to confront exams. Because exams are different, I have devoted the final chapter of the book to them.

50

Preparing for and Taking Exams and High-Stakes Tests

Dear Teacher,

Do I study for exams the same way I study for quizzes and tests?

Sincerely,

Fretting About Exams

Dear Fretting,

There are really two types of exams that students take: those that are usually written by the teacher and given at the end of a term, and those that are written by an outside group of testers, the so-called high-stakes tests. I'll begin by giving you strategies for exams that are written by your teacher.

My answer to your question is yes . . . and no. The prospect of studying for exams can be daunting. When you are faced with upcoming exams, there appears to be so much to do and so little time in which to do it. Furthermore, you are probably faced with exams in several subjects that you will take one after the other. The fact is, however, you will use precisely the same skills you have been learning from this book; you will simply pace yourself a little differently.

Start preparing early—much earlier than you did for your tests. Most students make the mistake of waiting until the teacher begins to review for the exams (or worse, until the weekend before the exams). This is far too late in the game. There is just too much to review and relearn. Waiting until the last minute creates unnecessary pressure and stress—and stress, as you now know, reduces the efficiency with which you study.

Well before review week, you should locate all of the materials you will need to prepare for the exam. Just as you did before a test, be sure you have all of your notes carefully organized into a single notebook. Keep it safe. You are responsible for making sure you have everything you will need; I do not know a single teacher who will be sympathetic if, after the exam, you say that the reason you did poorly is because someone took your notebook. Do not leave your papers or textbooks lying around at school.

Now that you have all the materials you will need to study, you can focus your energy on preparing for the exams themselves. You already know how to prepare a study schedule. Block out time each night for exam review. Initially, you will study for your exam in addition to all of your regular homework. Study for each exam a little bit every night, gradually increasing the amount of time you devote to preparing for the exams. When you prepare your exam review schedule, also write down the actual topics in every course that you intend to study each night. In this way, you will map out how you plan to complete your homework as well as review all of the material. As always, discuss your schedule with your family so that everyone is aware of the demands that have been placed on you and can be supportive.

All of the same rules about study schedules and focused study that you have already learned apply to exams. By now, you know whether you should begin with those topics and skills you know well or with the parts that gave you the greatest amount of trouble.

Do not be put off if your friends have not started studying yet. Your study schedule is unique to you. Maybe you need a bit more time than your friends do in order to master the material. Perhaps they are not as responsible as you about their work and do not know how to study. One of the biggest pitfalls comes when a student who lacks confidence watches what others are doing and begins to have self-doubt. Stick with your program. You used it on unit tests, and you know it works.

You already know that you need to be an active listener in class. Teachers often give hints about what to expect on the exam. Find out what the exam will cover and be sure to ask about its format. Modify your exam preparation accordingly.

There is a trap that you need to avoid when you turn to your old tests and quizzes. Students who do not know any better try to memorize the questions and answers that the teacher had asked. This is an ineffective technique because teachers do not always ask the same question on an exam. They might rephrase the question or even present it in a new light that touches on concepts taught in different units. Instead of memorizing old questions, make a note of those topics and areas that were difficult for you, and then give them extra attention as you study for the exam. Do not write down the entire question; just jot down the topic. Next, look at those areas you seemed to know for the test but have now forgotten. Record those topics, too, so you can refresh your memory.

Should you talk with students who took the course last year? Absolutely! Pick their brains about what the exam was like. Was it hard? Did it have a lot of multiple-choice questions? How was it graded? The more you know about an exam, the better you can prepare for it. This is not cheating. You did not ask about actual questions (the students probably could not remember them, anyway). You just wanted to find out what *kind* of exam to expect. The more you know, the more confident you will be.

Try to get enough exercise and sleep during the review process. Staying up extremely late in order to study is foolish because internalizing information is harder when you are tired. You might have to give up some of your social activities during this period of exam review so that you will have enough energy to concentrate on your studies. Get up early enough on the day of the exam so your brain is fully active by the time you sit down to take it. Remember to eat a good breakfast. Come to class early so you will not be in a panic. Go to the bathroom before the exam so you do not lose precious time while you are taking it. Find a comfortable chair and set up your workplace. Bring plenty of presharpened pencils so you do not waste time getting up and sharpening them during the exam. Unless you are required to use a pen, I recommend using a pencil because it is easier to erase your mistakes. It's a good idea to bring a watch on the day of the exam. You may not be able to see the clock in the exam room, and you will need to be able to pace yourself. If you will need one, be sure you have a calculator (with fresh batteries!).

Other students will be anxious and may be frantically asking each other last-minute questions about topics they do not think they know. Do not get caught up in that frenzy. It will just make you doubt yourself, and you will be nervous when you start to take your exam.

Remember to pace yourself as you take the exam. Take a minute to preread it. Read the directions very carefully. Look for directives. Take periodic stretch breaks. Remember your essay-writing rules. Leave plenty of space so you can return to your answers if you want to add to them later. If you are unsure of an answer, skip it. Come back to it later.

When you have answered the last question, go back and check your answers, but do not waste time looking at all of them. As you take the exam, make a mark by those questions for which you are absolutely sure about your answer. Then, when you review your answers, look back over only those questions that have not been marked.

Later, when the exam is returned to you, look it over just as you would any test. As you check your answers and see how you did, ask yourself if you think you were fully prepared for the exam. Now that you know what the exam was like, would you have studied any differently? Did you use your time wisely while you took the exam? Did you follow the directions? Did you answer the correct number of essay questions? Did you make any careless errors? If so, how can you avoid making them next time? Learn from this experience and adjust the way in which you prepare for your exams.

All exams weigh heavily upon the life of a student, but some are especially stressful. They are the so-called high-stakes tests. Examples include state-mandated testing programs, the results of which are especially important to districts, schools, and teachers; the SATs (Scholastic Assessment Tests) and ACTs (originally, ACT was the acronym for American College Testing, but now it is officially just ACT), which measure students' knowledge and abilities at the end of high school and which, therefore, are often scrutinized by college admissions teams; and the Advanced Placement exams, which give high school students the opportunity to earn college credit and which also give college admissions departments a way to measure students' achievement in each subject area.

I think the worst part about high-stakes tests is the anxiety they produce. As you now know, anxiety interferes with the ability to prepare for and take a test. Luckily, you have learned many effective study strategies that will reduce your anxiety and keep you in command of the situation. You can start preparing for a high-stakes test as soon as it is announced. As you did with the other type of exam described earlier, find out from your teacher as much as you can about the test. Some companies publish information about their tests and even release old tests that you can take for practice. You may find out if your local bookstore or library carries books that are specifically designed to help you prepare for your test. This information is useful. It will help you decide how you should prepare for the test. Find out if it is divided into sections and how long each one takes. This knowledge will help you decide how to pace yourself as you take the test. Find out if you will be penalized for guessing at answers. If not, you should guess the answer to every question that you cannot answer. The more you know about the test, the less frightening it will seem to you. Knowing effective strategies is the greatest way to reduce anxiety.

You might take this test at an entirely different school. If so, do not let the new setting make you nervous. If you need them, remember to bring any registration papers that you may have been given as well as proper ID when you report to the test center and sign in. When you walk into the test room, find a seat in a well-lit area and relax. Do a few stretching exercises while quietly sitting in your seat. Stretch and then relax your muscles, one limb at a time—first your left leg, and then your right, and so on. Take a few deep breaths to bring oxygen to your brain. While you take the test, practice all of the test-taking strategies you have learned. When you are given a break, stand up and move around to get your circulation going.

These tests are more anxiety-provoking than "ordinary" exams not only because so much rides on their results, but also because they are often the first exams students take that are written, scored, and judged entirely by outsiders with whom the students have no contact. More and more, high-stakes tests are using a combination of multiple-choice and free-response questions. The essays are read and scored by strangers, not by a teacher whose preferences you know. Instead of merely asking students to write about what they know about a subject, these essay questions often ask students to state and support a thesis, interpret data, or describe how to solve a problem. The art of writing an answer for these questions revolves around the word *focus*.

Begin your essay with a short, highly focused introductory paragraph. Remember: you should not repeat the question. Instead, give a clear thesis statement. State your main point, position, or argument. Imagine you were asked to explore the causes of the Revolutionary War. You might write a concise sentence such as, "The roots of the Revolutionary War can be traced to the early settlements at Plymouth and the Massachusetts Bay Colony." In an articulate sentence, demonstrate that you understand the nature of the problem or what the data involved. For example, if you are presented with a table and a graph that are to be used to analyze the validity of a hypothesis, you might write, "Observations were made of the average speed of a cart rolling down a ramp that was placed at increasingly steeper angles in order to determine whether the speed of an object is affected by the amount of kinetic energy placed in that object." Not only do you send a signal to the reader that you really understood the question, your well-focused sentence will also keep you on track as you write, preventing you from moving off on too many tangents.

Do not give any supporting information in your introductory paragraph. That will come later. Keep this paragraph simple. On an essay test, especially, it is better to write one powerful sentence than to write several that are weak and wordy. In any event, do not write more than just a few sentences. You really do not want to spend too much time on this paragraph; move as quickly as you can into the main part of your answer.

In the main body of your essay, be sure to give evidence that supports your thesis statement. Refer to the data to support your analysis. Define your terms and use examples that you have learned in your courses. Once you have made your point, move on.

Many students find concluding paragraphs to be difficult to write. I have some simple suggestions. Do not spend valuable time restating what you wrote in your introductory paragraph. Instead, write about the *significance* of the answer you have written in your essay. What are the consequences of the things you have written? You might even suggest a question that follows naturally from your answer. Is there a connection between the phenomenon you wrote about and your daily life? If you cannot think of anything to say in a concluding paragraph, I recommend that you just stop writing. You will receive more points by writing a strong essay that has no conclusion than by weakening it with a final paragraph that does not say anything.

Fretting, you asked a really good question. Regardless of the type of exam you face, I am sure you will agree with other students: the hardest part of an exam lies in its preparation. If you learn to prepare well for your exams, you're bound to succeed. Good luck!

References

Baker, J. R. (2005). *Is multiple-column online text better? It depends!* Retrieved July 8, 2006, from http://psychology.witchita.edu/surl/usabilitynews/72/columns/htm

Barkley, R. A. (2000, August). Genetics of childhood disorders XVII. ADHD, part I: The executive functions and ADHD. *Journal of the American Academy of Child and Adolescent Psychiatry, 38,* 1064–1070.

Berkhoff, F. (2005). *Lose weight overnight.* Retrieved January 2, 2006, from http://chealth.canoe.ca

Bower, J. M., & Parsons, L. M. (2003, August). Rethinking the "lesser brain." *Scientific American, 289,* 51–57.

Cahill, L., & McGaugh, J. (1995, December). A novel determination of enhanced memory associated with emotional arousal. *Conscious Cognition, 4,* 410–421.

Cahill, L., Prins, B., Weber, M., & McGaugh, J. (1994, October). β-adrenergic activation and memory for emotional events. *Nature, 371,* 702–704.

Carraway, K. (2003, April). *How neuroscience informs and influences teaching.* Presentation at the Learning and the Brain Conference, Cambridge, MA.

Cherry, E. C. (1953). Some experiments on the recognition of speech, with one and with two ears. *Journal of Acoustic Society of America, 25,* 975–979.

Conyers, M., & Wilson, D. (2001). *Just do it: Putting brain research to work in the classroom.* Presentation at the Learning and the Brain Conference, Washington, DC.

Cooper, H. (1994). Homework research and policy: A review of the literature. *Research Practice Newsletter.* Retrieved July 20, 2006, from http://education.umn.edu/carl/Reports/Rpractice/Summer94/homework.html

Cowan, N. (2001). *The magical number 4 in short-term memory: A reconsideration of mental storage capacity.* Retrieved July 25, 2006, from http://bbsonline.cup.cam.ac.uk

Defense mechanisms. (n.d.). Retrieved July 23, 2006, from http://www.planetpsych.com

De Fina, P. (2003, April). *How memory works and ways to improve it.* Presentation at the Learning and the Brain Conference, Cambridge, MA.

Family nutrition. (n.d.). Retrieved July 26, 2006, from http://www.askdrsears.com

Fishback, J. J. (1999). Learning and the brain. *Adult Learning, 10,* 18–22.

Foster, D. J., & Wilson, M. A. (2006, March 30). Reverse replay of behavioral sequences in hippocampal place cells during the awake state. *Nature 440,* 680–683.

Goldberg, E. (2003, April). *The executive brain: Gender, frontal lobes, and decision-making.* Presentation at the Learning and the Brain Conference, Cambridge, MA.

Greenleaf, R. K., & Levine, D. (2001). *How does emotion affect learning?* Presentation at the Learning and the Brain Conference, Washington, DC.

Gur, R. C. (2002, October). *Sex differences in learning.* Presentation at the Learning and the Brain Conference, Cambridge, MA.

Gurian, M., & Stevens, K. (2005). *The mind of boys: Saving our sons from falling behind in school and life.* San Francisco: Jossey-Bass.

Hallowell, E. M., & Ratey, J. J. (1994). *Driven to distraction.* New York: Pantheon.

Healey, J. M. (1990). *Endangered minds: Why children don't think and what we can do about it.* New York: Touchstone.

Hobson, A. (2003, April). *Sleep, memory, and learning.* Presentation at the Learning and the Brain Conference, Cambridge, MA.

Howard, P. J. (2006). *The owner's manual for the brain: Everyday application from mind–brain research* (3rd ed.). Austin: Bard Press.

Huitt, W. (2003). *The information processing approach to cognition.* Valdosta, GA: Valdosta State University. Retrieved July 20, 2006, from http://chiron.valdosta.edu

Jensen, E. (1997). *Brain-compatible strategies.* San Diego, CA: The Brain Store.

Jensen, E. (1998). *Teaching with the brain in mind.* Alexandria, VA: Association for Supervision and Curriculum Development.

Jensen, E. (2000, November). Moving with the brain in mind. *Educational Leadership, 58,* 34–37.

LeDoux, J. (1996). *The mysterious underpinnings of emotional life.* New York: Simon & Schuster.

Leiner, H. C., & Leiner, A. L. (2002). *The treasure at the bottom of the brain.* Retrieved February 8, 2006, from http://www.newhorizons.org

Lenoir, T., & Lowood, H. (n.d.). *Theaters of war: The military-entertainment complex.* Retrieved July 22, 2006, from http://www.stanford.edu/class/sts145/Library/Lenoir-Lowood_TheatersOfWar.pdf

Leonard, J. (2005). Helping the child with a learning block. *The Basic Educator, 23,* 1–2.

Levine, M. (2002). *Educational care: A system for understanding and helping children with learning differences at home and in school.* Cambridge, MA: Educators Publishing Service.

Pollitt, E., & Matthews, R. (1998). Breakfast and cognition: An integrative summary. *American Journal of Clinical Nutrition, 67,* 804S–813S.

Powell, C. A., Walker, S. P., Chang, S., & Grantham-McGregor, S. M. (1998). Nutrition and education: A randomized trial of the effects of breakfast in rural primary school children. *American Journal of Clinical Nutrition, 68,* 873–879.

Psychological self-help tools—online self-help book. (n.d.). Chapter 5, Changing behavior and thought. Retrieved July 24, 2006, from http://mhnet.org

Ratey, J. J. (2000, April). *The care and feeding of the brain.* Presentation at the Learning and the Brain Conference, Cambridge, MA.

Ratey, J. J. (2001). *A user's guide to the brain: Perception, attention, and the four theaters of the brain.* New York: Pantheon.

Ruben, C. G. (2002, October). *Sex differences in learning.* Presentation at the Learning and the Brain Conference, Cambridge, MA.

Sapolsky, R. (2003, September). Taming stress. *Scientific American, 289,* 87–95.

Schenck, J., & Kosik, K. S. (2000). *Using brain research to reshape classroom practice.* Presentation at the Learning and the Brain Conference, Cambridge, MA.

Schlaug, G., Jancke, L., & Pratt, H. (1995). In vivo evidence of structural brain asymmetry in musicians. *Science, 276,* 699–701.

Short term (working) memory. (n.d.). Retrieved July 21, 2006, from http://www.dc.peachnet.edu

Siegel, J. M. (2003, November). Why we sleep: The reasons that we sleep are gradually becoming less enigmatic. *Scientific American, 289,* 92–97.

Simons, D. J., & Chabris, C. F. (1999). Gorillas in our midst: Sustained inattentional blindness for dynamic events. *Perception, 28,* 1059–1074.

Society for Neuroscience. (2003). *Sleep and learning.* Retrieved July 24, 2006, from http://www.sfn.org.

Sousa, D. A. (2001). *How the brain learns: A classroom teacher's guide* (2nd ed.). Thousand Oaks, CA: Corwin Press.

Sprenger, M. (1999). *Learning and memory: The brain in action.* Alexandria, VA: Association for Supervision and Curriculum Development.

User interface design update: Reading. (2000, August). Retrieved July 22, 2006, from http://www.keller.com/articles/readingspeed.html

Wagner, A. (2002, May 9–11). *Memory: Multiple routes to remembering.* Presentation at Learning and the Brain Conference, Cambridge, MA.

Wolfe, P. (2001a). *Brain matters: Translating research into classroom practice.* Alexandria, VA: Association for Supervision and Curriculum Development.

Wolfe, P. (2001b). *Brain research and education: Fad or foundation?* Retrieved July 22, 2006, from http://www.mcli.dist.maricopa.edu/forum/fall03/brain.html

Wolfe, P. (2003). *The adolescent brain: A work in progress.* Retrieved October 23, 2005, from http://www.patwolfe.com

Wolfe, P. (2005). Advice for the sleep deprived. *Educational Leadership, 62,* 39–40.

Yurgelun-Todd, D. A. (1999, November). Adolescent decision making—emotions vs. reason. Presentation at the Learning and the Brain Conference, Cambridge, MA.

Zelago, P. D. (2005, June). The development of executive function across the lifespan. *About Kids Health.* Retrieved July 24, 2006, from http://www.aboutkidshealth.ca

Zinsser, W. (1990). *On writing well: An informal guide to writing nonfiction* (4th ed.). New York: Harper Perennial.

Index

CORWIN PRESS

The Corwin Press logo—a raven striding across an open book—represents the union of courage and learning. Corwin Press is committed to improving education for all learners by publishing books and other professional development resources for those serving the field of PreK–12 education. By providing practical, hands-on materials, Corwin Press continues to carry out the promise of its motto: **"Helping Educators Do Their Work Better."**